Matandani:
the Second Adventist Mission in

Malawi

Dedication

To God Almighty, who makes impossible things possible.

To my late father, Hisbon David Matemba (1944-1993), who loved knowledge.

To my daughter, Michelle Muthoni, whose life is the very existence of God's miracle.

Matandani:
the Second Adventist Mission in Malawi

Yonah Matemba

Kachere Theses no. 1

Copyright 2005 Yonah Matemba

All rights reserved. No part of this publication may be reproduced, stored in a retrieval system or transmitted in any form or by any means, electronic, mechanical, photocopying, recording or otherwise, without prior permission from the publishers.

Published by the
Kachere Series
P.O. Box 1037, Zomba, Malawi
ISBN 99908-76-00-2 (Kachere Theses no. 1)
[MA, University of Malawi, 2000]

First published 2005
Distributed outside Africa by
African Books Collective
http://www.africanbookscollective.com

Layout: Marie-Claire Muir and Mercy Chilunga
Cover Design: Marie-Claire Muir

Printed by Lightning Source

Acknowledgments

NO STUDY CAN ENTIRELY BE THE EFFORT OF A SINGLE PERSON and this study is no exception. Like many studies of this nature, many people contributed in various ways to the success of this study. As is often the case, unfortunately, it is not always possible to singularly thank all people who in various ways make such studies possible. To all people who have made this study possible, I express my gratitude. I would like to thank the staff in the Department of Theology and Religious Studies at Chancellor College, University of Malawi for providing advice and encouragement during the writing and presentation of this thesis.

I must acknowledge gratefully the assistance that my supervisors, Dr Klaus Fiedler, gave me at every stage of the research and more so for his patience and constructive criticisms. I am particularly thankful to him for taking the risk in believing that I could survive the programme and for part of the assistance that enabled me to buy research equipment and make research trips to Matandani mission, and also, for indirectly teaching me that in life we can do the impossible in a 24-hour period.

Further expression of gratitude is due to Mr. Samuel Machilika, Registrar of Matandani Mission Secondary School where the bulk of the research was done, for giving me unlimited access to files, papers and introducing me to key informants. Concerning accommodation and meals during the period of my research at Matandani mission, my thanks extend to the entire Machilika family. In particular, I would like to thank Mrs. Machilika for warming bathing water for me in the cold mornings and for her well-prepared meals.

To the two main oral informants of this study, Mr. F.L. Matsimbe and Mr. S.J. Kaphale, I extend utmost gratitude. Not only did they answer my lengthy and at times ambiguous questions, but also they took an honest interest in my research. I would like to express my indebtedness to Ms. Sandra Konigmacher for much of the life sketch of Samuel Konigmacher. I would also like to thank the staff at the Malawi National Archives office in Zomba and the Ellen G. White Branch office at Andrews University, USA for materials that have been used in this study.

Finally, I would like to acknowledge with appreciation Mr P. Sosola for supplying a photograph of Pr Yokoniah Sosola that has been used in this book. The other illustrations are mine.

Yonah Hisbon Matemba
July 2003

Contents

Introduction	15

Chapter 1
Mission Foundations 1908-1915 — 25
  Origins of Seventh-day Adventists in Malawi — 25
  Beginnings of Matandani Mission, 1907-1908 — 29
  Establishment of Matandani Mission, 1908-1914 — 35
  Impact of the Chilembwe Rising of 1915 — 46

Chapter 2
Regular Mission Work 1915-1939 — 53
  Second Wave of Missionary and National Workers, 1915-1939 — 53
  The Wilfred Gudu Affair, 1922-1925 — 65

Chapter 3
Institutional Development 1943-1971 — 77
  The Work of O.I. Fields, 1943-1967 — 77
  African Teachers' Protest of 1953 — 86
  Industrial Training School, 1953-1971 — 94
  End of the Missionary Ear, 1968-1971 — 100

Chapter 4
The Ear of National Leadership, 1971-1989 — 103
  Rationale for Indigenization in the Adventist Church — 103
  Triumphs of National Leadership, 1971-1989 — 109
  Adventist Churches in Neno: Weathering "Folk Churches" — 113
  Impact of Indigenization, 1977-1989 — 117

Conclusion — 131

Appendices — 137
  Notes on Notable Oral Informants — 137
  List of Mission Directors and Principals — 139
  Industrial School Student Enrolment (1953-1989) — 140

Bibliography
Primary Sources 143
   Oral Informants 143
   Archival Sources – Malawi National Archives, Zomba (MNA) 145
Secondary Sources 147
   Unpublished 147
   Published 148

Illustrations

MAPS

Map 1. Adventist Missions in Malawi, 1902-1950   12

Map 2. Sketch plan of Matandani Mission   13

Map 3. Adventist Churches in the Matandani Mission area   114

TABLES

Table 1. Some Out-Schools Operated by Matandani Mission (c.1923) 58

FIGURES

Fig. 1 Pastor Yokoniah Sosola   63

Fig. 2 The Industrial Training School building   99

Glossary of Chichewa Terms

Chichewa	The lingua franca of Malawi.
gogo	Grandparent
Kachipande	Nickname given to the proprietor of Banga Estate by his workers for his habit of beating his workers using a cane.
kaliyoni	Literally translated from the English phrase "carry on".
machila	Portable hammock carried by porters. This was the means of transport for most early white settlers and travelers in colonial Malawi.
mlangamfiti	Literary translated as "punisher of wizards/witches" meaning, punishing the evil one.
Mnyamatandani	Literally translated as "who is the man who can withstand the toil?"
msonkhano wa misasa	Literary meaning "meeting held in temporary dwellings." This is the annual Adventist camp meeting.
nsembe	Ancestral sacrifices.

Abbreviations

AFL	African Lakes Corporation
AG	Assemblies of God
CCAP	Church of Central Africa Presbyterian
CS	Church of Scotland
DC	District Commissioner
DRC	Dutch Reformed Church
EAD	Eastern Africa Division
EWEP	Ellen G. White Estate Papers
GC	General Conference (of the Seventh-day Adventist Church)
MiP	Miscellaneous Papers
MNA	Malawi National Archives
MP	Matandani Papers
MU	Malawi Union
MUMP	Malawi Union Matandani Papers
MwP	Mpingo wa Baptist
RC	Roman Catholic Church
SDA	Seventh-day Adventist Church
SDB	Seventh-day Baptist Church
SEAU	South East Africa Union
TC	Topia Church
WTM	Watch Tower Movement
ZIM	Zambezi Industrial Mission

Arrangement of Sources

The mass of primary data used in the study has been arranged and named in the following way: Materials found at Matandani Mission are Matandani Papers (MP). Materials found at the Malawi Union are Malawi Union Matandani Papers (MUMP). Materials from the Ellen G. White Estate branch office at Andrews University in America are Ellen White Estate Papers (EWEP). Those from the Malawi National Archives in Zomba, maintain the standard abbreviation, (MNA). Finally, Materials that do not fall into any of the above-mentioned categories have been classified as Miscellaneous Papers (MiP).

Map 1: Adventist Missions in Malawi (1902-1950)

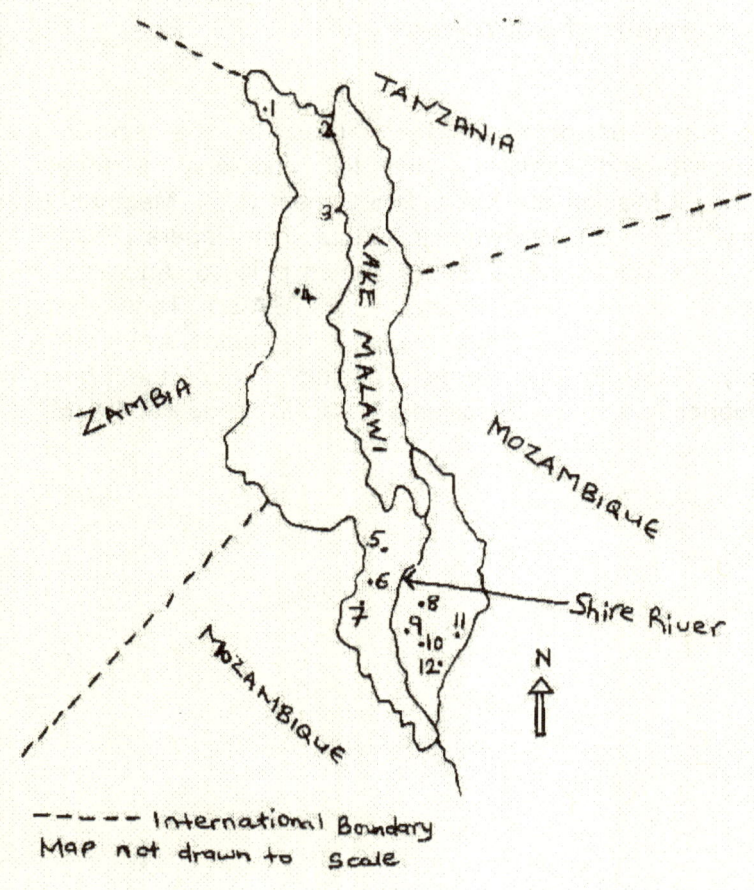

1. Chambo Mission (1949)
2. Ighembe Mission (1935)
3. Luwazi Mission (1929)
4. Lunjika Mission (1929)
5. Lakeview Mission (1934)
6. Matandani Mission (1908)
7. Thambani Mission (1929)
8. Zomba Mission
9. Chileka Mission
10. Malamulo Mission (1902)
11. Chinyama Mission (1936)
12. Thekerani Mission (1924)

Map 2: Sketch Plan of Matandani Mission

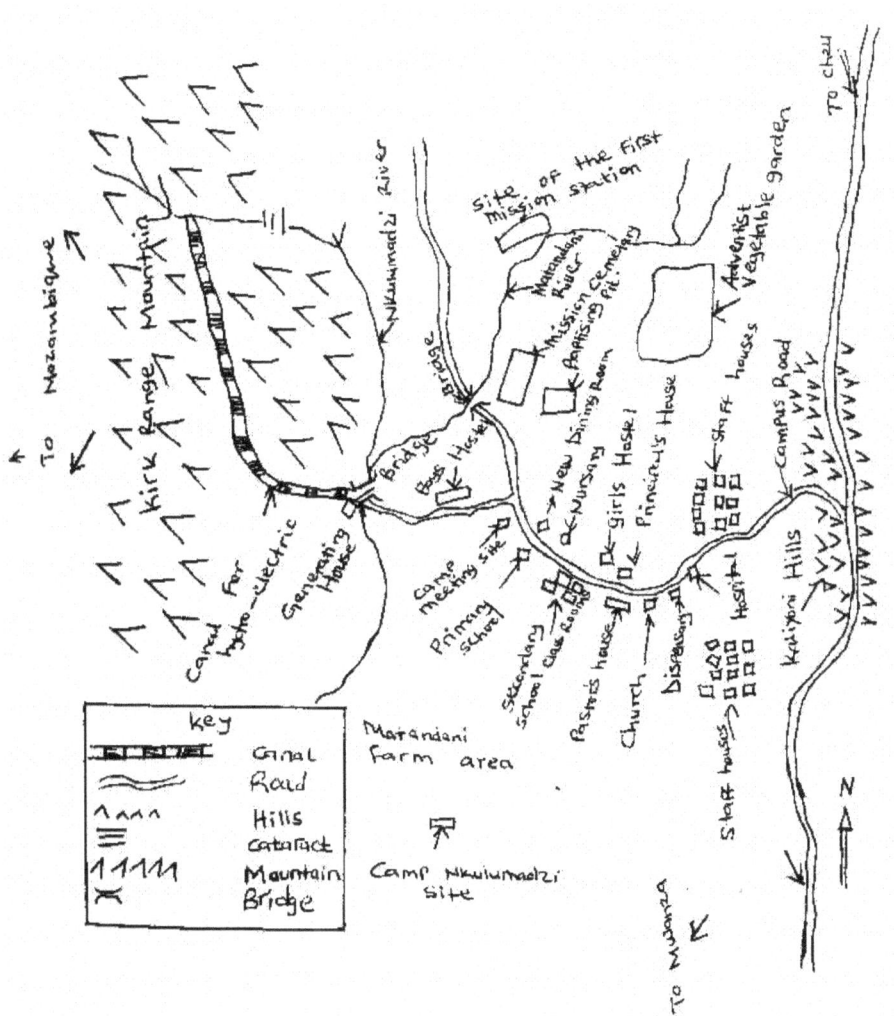

Introduction

The contribution of Matandani mission to Adventist work between 1908 and 1989 through evangelization and especially education was felt in Malawi and beyond. In the late 1950s and early 1960s in particular, students from as far as Botswana, Uganda and Rwanda came to attend its industrial training school. In the periphery of the mission, a number of out-schools and churches were established. As its evangelical and educational out-reach expanded, areas further from the mission saw the opening up of new mission stations. By early 1960, most of the Neno area and Mwanza district had felt the influence of the mission.

The choice of Matandani Mission as a subject for research was influenced by the fact that this mission, although a contemporary of Malamulo Mission whose story is relatively known, that of Matandani Mission is not, notwithstanding the contribution the mission made to the overall SDA work in Malawi. Again, since 1908 when Matandani Mission was established, no other SDA mission was established until 1924 when Thekerani, an outstation of Malamulo, was established.

It is the purpose of this thesis to provide material for and analysis of the history of Matandani mission. The analysis begins in 1908 when the mission was established and terminates in 1989 when the decline of the mission was signified by the closure of the mission's industrial training school. The study traces and examines the origins, development and decline of an Adventist mission in Africa. The decline of this mission, sadly, is a paradigm of the current state of many Adventist missions in Africa since the advent of indigenization.

Research Issues

This thesis mainly covers four broad issues. First, it outlines the genesis of Matandani mission. By analyzing oral sources of the people in the area where the mission was established, a picture of the area before and soon after the arrival of Adventists emerges. This oral data challenges the general view that only missionaries were active participants in the development of missions like Matandani. This study is an attempt to give recognition to the African contribution in the history of the mission. The second issue involves the recognition of the immense missionary contribution at the mission. While not all missionaries were industrious, the study shows that through the personal efforts of some missionaries, the mission developed to an admirable level not only for Adventists in Malawi but in the entire Eastern Africa Division (EAD).[1]

Thirdly, there is a recurring bias by church historians who are themselves members of the churches their researches are based on. These tend to play down controversial issues and over-emphasize the positive attributes of their subject matter. For example, in exploring the conflict that occurred between the Seventh-day Adventist church and the remnants of the Seventh-day Baptist church in northern Malawi, Jaspine Bilima, an Adventist pastor, concluded that an amicable solution to both sides was reached. However, this assertion was made in spite of the fact that by the time Bilima did his research, there was archival evidence pointing to the fact that the conflict left many SDB members concerned, bitter.[2] By allowing the results of research tell the Matandani mission

---

[1] The hierarchical structure of the SDA church starts at its headquarters called the General Conference (GC), located in Washington, USA. Under it are Divisions found in continental areas of the world. Sometimes due to cultural or linguistic differences, a continent may further be subdivided. Then there are Unions found in countries. Unions are made up of a number of Fields or Conferences. A number of local churches in a particular area make up a Field or a Conference. All heads of these structures except the churches hold the title of president. The Malawi Union is in the Eastern African Division (EAD). The EAD offices are in Harare, Zimbabwe. Other countries in the EAD are Zimbabwe, Botswana, Zambia, Tanzania, Uganda, Kenya, Eritrea and Ethiopia.

[2] This issue requires further research. See Jaspine Bilima, "The Seventh-day Adventist Church in Malawi, 1900-1980," MDiv, Andrews University, 1987, p. 50. The primary data at the archives indicate the seriousness of this conflict. The archival materials where the issue is

story, this study has tried to avoid such temptations by showing that the history of this mission has both "smooth" and "rough" sides. Between 1915 and 1953 for example, the mission went through "trying times" when it was accused by the government of harboring Chilembwe dissidents and when it faced internal popular discontent by its African workers.

The last issue covered is the impact of national leadership on the development of the mission. Indigenization was a factor that largely contributed to problems the mission faced by 1989. The national workers who had earlier contributed to the establishment and early development of the mission, allowed the mission to decline when mission leadership was placed in their hands. The circumstances that contributed to this development are examined.

State of Research

This study is part of a research contribution to the history of the Adventist church in Malawi, a subject that has received little attention, in spite of the fact that the church has been in Malawi for about a century. Unfortunately for the church, much of its history remains in people's memories and in archives. Sadly, the first generation of Malawian Adventist workers (even those that could write) did not leave any substantial written records. There is the danger again that the second generation of these workers, many of whom are in old age, will die before their version of the church's rich past is recorded. This is the challenge that subsequent researchers into the SDA church in Malawi have and as a matter of urgency, such research should be undertaken. Although not directly relating to Matandani mission, there are some materials about the church that are found at the Malawi National Archives (MNA) and the Malawi Collection in the University of Malawi library, both in Zomba. A few written materials on aspects of the church's history in Malawi are found in some Adventist Universities and archival institutions in America and this location makes these materials difficult to access.

---

recorded are in the following MNA files: 52/624/29, 51/485, L3/33/5, 51/485/19, NN/19/1 and 542/1/2/1. These files are about the conflict between the SDA church and the SDB remnants in northern Malawi.

18   INTRODUCTION

There are however, a few unpublished studies focusing on various aspects of the activities of the church in the last one hundred years. Most of these studies focus on Malamulo mission, the church's first centre and for many synonymous with Adventism in Malawi. Cedric Khanje[3] analyses the evangelical impact of Malamulo mission in southern Malawi while S.K. Sayenda[4] looks at the contribution of the Adventist missionaries in the provision of medical services at Malamulo mission. Three other studies dealing with aspects of the church were written by E.P.P. Murowa,[5] Jaspine Bilima[6] and S.K. Yokasi.[7] Murowa's study examines the work of an Adventist pastor, Albert Kambuwa, the first study to give serious attention to the work of a Malawian Adventist worker. This interest in the study of the work of national workers was followed by Bilima whose study focuses on the pastoral work of James Malinki, one of the early African pastors in the church in Malawi. Finally, the study by Yokasi focuses on Adventists and education. The provision of education by the church through its schools scattered throughout the country is one area that the church has contributed to the development of human resources in Malawi.

One document that attempted to cover the history of the church in Malawi is a document found at both Malawi National Archives and at Ellen G. White Estate Branch Office at Andrews University. Titled, "History of the South East Africa Union" and written in 1952, this is the first attempt to outline the history of the church. It is weak on two points. The first one is that the study does not critically analyze Adventist issues but merely presents a topical outline of the church's events up to the 1950s. The second and more serious weakness is that the contribution

---

[3]   Cedric Khanje, "Impact of Malamulo Mission in Southern Malawi, Thyolo 1902-1972: A Broad Perspective," Seminar Paper, Chancellor College, University of Malawi, 1972.

[4]   S.K. Sayenda, "Missionaries and Health: The Case of Malamulo Mission Hospital, 1907-1964," History Seminar Paper, Chancellor College, University of Malawi, 1990.

[5]   E.P.P. Murowa, "Reverend Albert Kambuwa: A Critical Analysis of His Writings," History Seminar Paper, Chancellor College, 1976-1977.

[6]   Jaspine Bilima, "James Malinki of Malawi: Church Leader in Cross-cultural Ministry," DMin, Andrews University, 1993.

[7]   S.K. Yokasi, "An Evaluation of Seventh-day Adventist Mission in the Education Field from 1907 to the present," Chancellor College, 1980.

of African workers is not covered. Where there is a mention of an African worker, they are not given names nor are the details of the work they did covered. This is in spite of the fact that by 1950; a number of prominent Africans had worked in the church, some of whom were pioneers of missions and leaders in the church.

A comparatively serious study to date on the history of the church is a masters degree dissertation by Jaspine Bilima titled, "History of the Seventh-day Adventist Church in Malawi 1900-1980."[8] The major weakness of Bilima's study is similar to that of the document cited above in that it merely presents an outline of the history of the church. Bilima's work does not cover specific SDA issues. Other themes of the church's history in the period he confined his study to are also not covered. Themes like the proliferation of Adventist missions, threat of independency, protests of African workers and indegenisation, to mention a few, are some of those not covered.

The autobiography of Morrison Malinki (the father of James Malinki noted above), the first African Adventist worker in Malawi, is brief and topical. Although the document, located at the MNA, does not contain substantial information about Malinki and his work, the few things it has mentioned, confirm the accuracy of some information in other studies about him. Another work that contains some information on the history of the church is S.G. Maxwell's, *I Loved Africa*. This is a booklet with the author's romanticist account of his stay as a missionary in Africa (between 1942 and 1953 he was president of the Malawi Union).

Two books, in the analysis of their themes, have mentioned some aspects of Adventist work in Malawi. George Shepperson and Thomas Price's book, *Independent African: John Chilembwe and the Origins, Setting and Significance of the Nyasaland Rising of 1915*,[9] has noted in some detail, issues relating to the origin of Adventist work in Malawi. This discussion is incidental to the theme of Christian missions' alleged involvement to the Chilembwe Rising of 1915. Another equally important book that covers a similar issue, is Harry Langworthy's, *"Africa for the*

---

[8] MDiv, Andrews University.

[9] Edinburgh: Edinburgh University Press, 1987; Blantyre: CLAIM-Kachere, 2000 (Kachere Monograph no. 13).

African: The Life of Joseph Booth.[10] These two books also discuss the activities of Morrison Malinki, Peter Nyambo and Filipo Chinyama (all early African Adventist workers), in relation to the government's suspicion that through them, the Adventist church was involved in the Rising.

In general, research on the history of Adventist missions in Malawi is a subject that has received little attention. This is in spite of the fact by 1950, the church had twelve missions, each complete with a farm, school (including a number of out-schools on the outskirts of the mission), church, dispensary and other institutional infrastructure like staff houses. There is need, therefore, for research on these missions to be done with the view to address several issues among them: how these missions were established (including personalities involved), possible problems encountered, some of the missions' success stories and finally, factors that led to the closure of most of the missions (today there are only four missions in full operation and these are: Malamulo, Matandani, Lakeview and Lunjika). A clear example of the lack of detailed research on the church is the fact that although aspects of Malamulo mission have appeared in some studies, its complete history remains unwritten.

The Matandani mission story reconstructed in this book has never been told before. What is of interest is that the findings of this study have revealed issues that dispell some misconceptions about the establishment of Adventist missions in Malawi. One flaw in the available scanty written sources is that missionaries are credited to have been solely responsible for the establishment of Adventist missions in Malawi – that is missionaries alone located areas for missions and generally entered those areas "unannounced." While this could be true of missions like Malamulo, this study has found out that Matandani mission was largely established through African initiative. However, a single research subject, as this one, is sometimes inadequate to counteract strongly held perceptions. Future research on other Adventist missions in Malawi will reveal whether the African contribution in the origin and development Matandani mission was the exception or the norm.

---

[10] CLAIM-Kachere: Blantyre: 1996.

Research methods

A number of research methods were used in this study. Primary sources, usually hailed as the "hallmark" of historical information, comprise a large percentage of the sources used.[11] First, archival materials from the MNA were used. What little archival data on Matandani mission is found there, is contained in a few files labeled "District Commissioner's Notes for Neno." The only information that was found and was used in this study is a list of out-schools, churches and other buildings at the mission between 1907 and 1931. Some information on Wilfred Gudu, a church worker but later breakaway leader of the independent church called "Ana a Mulungu Church" is also found at the archives. Archival information on Gudu as was relevant to the Matandani mission story was also used in this study. The researcher also made inquiries at the Ellen G. White Research Center in Michigan, USA for any materials on the mission. Most of the data that was provided was from Adventist periodicals like *SDA Year Book*, *The Advent Review and the Sabbath Herald* and *Adventist Review*. However, the literature in these publications does not contain substantial information directly related to Matandani mission.

Had my research taken place before 1998 at Matandani mission, the study could have made use of the substantial amount of letters, documents and memos of the mission from its inception in 1908 to the present date. However, by the time the topic was chosen and approved by the university in May 1998, most materials on the mission had been destroyed. In June or July 1998, the building where all documents and papers of the mission had been stored had its roof blown away by heavy winds. Not having a place to store them while repair work could be undertaken, the mission administration decided to destroy them. In fact, for a long time the mission administration had wanted to destroy this mass of papers that appeared of little use to them. Added to this, it was felt that the papers were consuming space. The destruction of church documents should be understood in the context of SDA church policy which allows official documents to be kept for a maximum of five years.

---

[11] Paul Leeds stresses that "in the search for historical truth, therefore, the researcher relies, if at all possible, upon only primary data." See *Practical Research: Planning and Design*, New York: Macmillan, 1985, p. 125.

After that period, it is up to institutions to keep or destroy them. Most materials (especially letters and reports) on Matandani mission that are occasionally sent to South Malawi Field and Malawi Union, these being regional and national offices respectively, were also destroyed as per this policy

Much of the primary written data used in this study is from letters and minutes found in two files at Matandani mission. For unknown reasons, these files, containing written data about the mission mainly from early 1970s to the present date, escaped the destruction mentioned above. Materials in these files are the only surviving written primary documents about the mission that were available to the author and extensively used in this study. A few documents found at the Malawi Union office (and were accessible to the writer) dated from 1987 to the present, were used.

Oral sources were extensively used in this study. The writer was the only researcher and conducted all interviews personally. Added to observation, both informal and formal in-depth interviews were the main research tools used. From 21 to 27 August 1998 and 28 to 29 December 1999, oral data was collected from a number of interviewees, both women and men. Retired and active church workers at the mission were those who were interviewed. The selection of these individuals was based on several considerations such as: availability, reliability of interviewee information (e.g. reliability of information given) and participation of interviewee in some issues investigated (e.g. as in the cases of Kaphale and Matsimbe). A tape recorder and a field notebook were the main research materials used. This oral information tremendously contributed to the African side of the Matandani mission story. For example, it revealed a side of Matandani mission never before made public. The 1953 African Teachers' Protest that almost developed into a major strike action was made available to the researcher by chance, when one of the interviewees volunteered to talk about the "strike". If he had not done so, I could not have known about it. Apart from the "strike," some biographical aspects of important African workers at the mission were obtained from the interviews. Another source that was used in this study, as was relevant to the themes in the study, was secondary sources such as books, dissertations and articles.

This study has allowed results of research to tell the Matandani story. Issues however controversial or unpopular to the ordinary Adventist view have been analyzed and presented as close to what happened as it was possible based on available sources. The advantages of studying one's own church are several. One, the researcher has insider knowledge of the subject under research, a fact that allows an informed interpretation of issues. Another advantage is that it is easier to gather data (especially oral and written primary) such as minutes and memos because church officials find it safe to give out information to persons they know and trust.

However, a researcher, who is also a member of the church he/she is researching on, is sometimes faced with the problem of selection, a dilemma common in historical research.[12] Usually the choice is to ignore some "uncomfortable" issues of one's church. However, this writer applied the positivist approach in the interpretation and reconstruction of the history of Matandani mission. According to John Tosh, the implication of the positivist approach to history is that

> the historian's first duty is to accumulate factual knowledge about the past – facts which are verified by applying critical method to the primary sources; those facts will in turn determine how the past should be explained or interpreted. In this process the beliefs and values of historians are irrelevant; their sole concern is with the facts and the generalizations to which they logically lead.[13]

The writer is a Seventh-day Adventist who believes that by being "true" to historical research, lessons of the past can help the church avoid repeating past mistakes.[14] Preston Monterrey, a Seventh-day Adventist pastor

---

[12] A discussion on the problems of selection is found in R.J. Atkinson, *Knowledge and Explanation in History: An Introduction to the Philosophy of History*, London: Macmillan, 1978, pp. 79-88.

[13] See The Pursuit of History: Aims, Methods and New Directions in the Study of Modern History, (second edition), London and New York: Longman, 1993, p. 132.

[14] Whether history can be objectively or subjectively written, is a matter of inexhaustible debate. Perhaps a historian can be said to be objective if the element of subjectivity in his/her analysis is less and vice-versa. On some discussion on the issue see Atkinson, *Knowledge and Explanation in History*, pp. 67-94.

has explained that "the failure to learn lessons from our past history" is a major problem facing Adventist work today.[15] This study is important in other ways too. To non-Adventist Christians in Malawi, the study shows that the disadvantages of indigenization in many evangelical Christian missions far outweigh its advantages. The study concludes that without the full participation of missionaries in the day-to-day affairs of many of these missions in Africa, the future and success of these missions is uncertain.

---

[15] Preston Monterrey, "Waco: Insights on the Davidian Movement Part I," *Our Firm Foundation*, vol. 8, no. 6, June 1993, pp. 14-15.

Chapter 1

MISSION FOUNDATIONS 1908-1915

Origins of Seventh-day Adventists in Malawi

The Seventh-day Adventist (SDA) church, an American evangelical Christian group, begun its missionary out-reach outside the United States in 1874 when J.N Andrews was sent to evangelize in Switzerland.[1] In Africa, the church made its early presence in Egypt first, in about 1878 and later in 1901. This northern penetration saw the evangelization of much of East Africa.[2] The second entry into Africa was through the

---

[1] The SDA church, an offshoot of the Millerite Movement, was formally organized in 1863 when Ellen G. White and her husband, James, organized the first church. William Miller, a Baptist minister, preached in the 1830s and 1840s that the Second Coming of Jesus to earth was to be real and the day exact. When Jesus did not come as predicted, many of his followers were greatly disappointed. Some of his followers embarked upon an intensive study of the Bible under the spiritual guidance of Ellen White. These were those who later became the modern Seventh-day Adventists. Since its inception, the church has held the view that Ellen White is a latter-day prophet. The church insists that Saturday and not Sunday is the biblical day of worship. Rebaptism and tithing are widely performed practices in the church. Even to this day, some people still classify the SDA church as a cult mainly because of its salient apocalyptic theology and the prophetic status it accords to Ellen G. White. For aspects of the historical development of the SDA church, see Ellen G. White, *The Great Controversy*, Ottawa: Pacific Press, 1993, pp. 217-228; J.N. Loughborough, *The Second Advent Movement: Its Rise and Progress*, Review and Herald Publishing Association, 1992, pp. 343 ff. For the view that the SDA church is considered by others a cult see Elijah Mvundura, "The Great Controversy: A Historiographical Review," (draft document) 1999, p. 1.

[2] See Baldur E. Pfeiffer, "The Coming of the Mission to East Africa", in Baldur E. Pfeiffer (ed.), *Seventh-day Adventist Contribution to East Africa, 1903-1983*, Frankfurt: Peter Lang, 1985, pp. 13-14.

southern tip of Africa. In 1885, an American Adventist convert named William Hunt who had earlier lived in Australia as a mineral prospector before relocating to the mining town of Kimberly in South Africa, introduced the Adventist faith in South Africa. This southern penetration facilitated the evangelization of much of southern Africa.[3] In 1902, twenty-eight years after J.N. Andrews' trip to Switzerland, the Adventist church began its work in Malawi, a country then under British rule and known as Nyasaland. The church could have been introduced in Malawi earlier. In 1893, James, George, a British citizen but American trained evangelist came to Malawi. While doing theological studies at Battle Creek College (today Andrews University) in USA, James was intrigued by the stories he read of the Scottish missionary-doctor, David Livingstone, whose exploits eventually opened up Central Africa and particularly Malawi, to Europeans. Livingstone's harrowing accounts of slave trade activities and the absence of Christianity in the area ultimately led to the British colonization of much of Central Africa.[4] James took upon the challenge and decided to come to Africa to introduce the Adventist message. He requested the GC for financial support for his evangelical trip to Africa but none was made available to him. Undeterred, James sold his little worldly possessions, boarded a ship and finally reached Malawi, the land David Livingstone had fondly described in his speeches and journals.[5]

James came into the country as a self-supporting missionary and when he arrived in Blantyre, he met the Baptist independent missionary, Joseph Booth, who did not hesitate to assist the lone missionary in every way possible. Booth even offered to give James one of the many plots of land he had acquired from the local chiefs, if the Adventist evangelist wanted to set up a mission. Booth's friendly disposition to James, an

---

[3] See Yonah Matemba, "Some Aspects of the History of the Seventh-day Adventists in Botswana from 1922 to 1970," *Botswana Notes and Records*, Volume 29, 1997, p. 23.

[4] David Livingstone is one of the British Christian missionaries in Africa whose work has been extensively covered. His first book about his work in Central Africa is a relevant source here. See David Livingstone, *Missionary Travels and Researches in South Africa*, London: John Murray, New York: Harper Brothers, 1858.

[5] For an account of the brief stay of George James in Malawi see Gordon Doss, "George James: Pioneer in Malawi Work", *Adventist Review*, 1993.

Adventist, was likely influenced by the fact that Booth had earlier met a group of Adventists in Cape Town, South Africa as he made his maiden trip to Central Africa. Booth arrived in Malawi in 1892, the same year Harry Johnston (first British Commissioner of Malawi) was struggling to set up the first British administration amidst a myriad of obstacles viz. Arab Slave-trade activities, Ngoni resentment of the British and the Nguru of Mozambique *en masse* immigration into southern Malawi.[6] The Adventists Booth met in South Africa astounded the Baptist missionary with their teachings especially the question of the Sabbath. As noted later in this section, this relationship between Booth and the Adventists is important for the fact that Booth established the first Adventist mission in Malawi.

In spite of James' continued financial request from the GC to start building a mission on the plot of land that Booth gave him, the GC's response remained negative. In 1894 James died from malaria on a steamer in the Shire River as he made his way to Solusi Mission in Bulawayo, Zimbabwe where he had heard that Adventist missionaries had arrived and had begun setting up a mission. The officially sanctioned entry of the church in Malawi, after the abrupt end of the evangelical attempt of George James, was unique. This entry was independent of the general expansion of Adventist missionary work in Africa either from its earliest point of entry in the north through Egypt or in the south through South Africa.[7] Even the founding of Solusi mission in 1894 had no direct bearing on the official entry of the church in Malawi.

Joseph Booth (1851-1932),[8] an enigmatic independent Baptist missionary, began the SDA work in Malawi.[9] Briefly, in 1900 Booth

---

[6] See Shepperson and Price, *Independent African*, pp. 11-12.

[7] For example, the entry of the church in East Africa i.e. Kenya, Ethiopia and Tanzania was because of the northern penetration. See Pfeiffer, "The coming of the mission to East Africa," pp. 13-14. For example, the entry of the church in much of Southern Africa i.e. South Africa, Zimbabwe, Lesotho and Botswana was because of the Southern penetration. See Matemba, "Some Aspects of the History of the Seventh-day Adventists in Botswana," p. 23.

[8] The story of Joseph Booth is interesting and extensive but only aspects relevant to Adventists will be mentioned. See Harry Langworthy, *"Africa for the African" The Life of Joseph Booth*, Blantyre: CLAIM-Kachere, 1996, pp. 161-173.

established Plainfield mission at Makwasa in southern Thyolo. This mission was under the auspices of Seventh-day Baptists (SDB) of Plainfield, New Jersey, USA. Two years later, the mission was sold to the SDA church through the influence of Booth. The first directors of the mission under Adventist control were Booth himself and an Adventist missionary, Thomas Branch an African American. Booth left the mission in 1903 either because of a deportation order by government or because of the differences that developed between him and Branch on how the mission was to be administered.[10] In 1907, Branch was replaced by Joel Cyrus Rogers whose work signaled a new era in the growth of Adventist work in Malawi.[11] Although Rogers left in 1912, subsequent directors of Adventist work in Malawi stationed at Malamulo mission and later in Blantyre, advanced the work. In fact, between 1908 and 1950 there was an unprecedented expansion of Adventist evangelical work throughout the country. It should be observed that much of this work was done by various African workers some of who were pioneers in the establishment of mission stations. For example, Roman Chimera and James Ngaiyaye established Thekerani and Thambani missions, respectively.[12]

---

[9] Apart from introducing the SDA work in the country, Booth was directly responsible for the establishment of four other Christian missions and indirectly; five other missions were established because of him. See J. Chaphadzika Chakanza, "Sectarianism in Joseph Booth's Mission Foundations, 1925-1975: The Search for Causative Factors," *Religion in Malawi*, number 2, volume 1, 1988, p. 6.

[10] Many writers have described Joseph Booth as a "religious hitchhiker" or a "maverick" missionary. Throughout his missionary work in Malawi he seemed to be changing church allegiance. When he broke ties with the SDB he "joined" the SDA while in America and managed to interest the church to engage him as their missionary. It is not clear from the sources available whether he was a member of the SDA church through either re-baptism or profession of faith, the two avenues to gain SDA membership of people from other denominations. I contend that Booth never was an Adventist because in the available sources there is no evidence showing that these two Adventist rites were ever performed on him when he "joined" the Adventist church. See Yonah Matemba, "Joseph Booth: A Critical Look at his Association with the Seventh-day Adventist Church in Malawi, 1892-1906" (unpublished.).

[11] It was Cyrus J. Rogers, who in 1907 changed the name Plainfield to Malamulo, the latter name meaning "commandments" in the *Chichewa* language. See EWEP "History of the South East Africa Union," 192 (no author), p. 10.

[12] Bilima, "The SDA in Malawi," pp. 42-43.

In all, by 1950 as the map of Malawi on page 11 shows, the Adventist church boasted twelve missions scattered mostly in the southern and northern parts of the country. From this map, it can be observed that Matandani mission (1908) besides the famous Malamulo mission (1902) was the center of Adventist work in Malawi until other Adventist missions were opened from 1924 onwards.[13]

Beginnings of Matandani Mission, 1907-1908

The SDA church established Matandani mission in Neno district as a response to a request for a school by the people of Chakulemeka village, living in the area where the mission is located. Much of the effort in interesting the church to come to the area was that of a local a convert from this village named Mark Chakachadza.[14] Chakachadza was a student at Malamulo Mission School in the years probably between 1903 and 1906. It was at Malamulo where Chakachadza was converted and baptized into the church. It is likely that during the time Chakachadza was at Malamulo, personalities like Philip Chinyama, Morrison Malinki and possibly Joseph Booth and Peter Nyambo (all whose activities and their relevance to the Matandani story are told in this book) were at the mission.

Mabel Branch, the grown up daughter of Thomas Branch, the first officially sent Adventist missionary to Malawi, started the first Adventist school at Malamulo in 1902. So successful was the school that after Morrison Malinki joined her in 1904, the school's total student enrollment reached sixty-six, twenty-four of whom were boarders.[15] Although Mabel Branch came to Malawi with her parents, her work in Malawi qualifies her for pioneer status as the first Adventist teacher in Malawi. Mabel Branch not only introduced the first Adventist school in Malawi but together with

---

[13] As already noted, although aspects of the history of Malamulo mission appear in some studies and have been quoted in this dissertation, the complete history of the mission remains largely unwritten.

[14] Unless otherwise stated, the story of Mark Chakachadza outlined in this study is based on the oral information of S.J. Kaphale, F.L. Matsimbe and Mrs. E. Kaphale (granddaughter of Mark Chakachadza), 25 August 1998 and 28 December 1999.

[15] Bilima, "The SDA in Malawi," p. 35.

Malinki for example, also pioneered in the translation of English Bible tracts into *Chichewa*. She was also helpful in translating her father's sermons and conversations into the vernacular, a language she learnt before her father.[16]

Towards the end of 1906 Mark Chakachadza, whose father was the headman of Chakulemeka village, went home to spend the school holidays there. While at home, Chakulemeka village residents led by the village headman, asked Mark Chakachadza to invite Adventist missionaries, stationed at Malamulo mission, then the centre of Adventist faith in the country, to come to the village and open a school. As they waited for Chakachadza to make that trip to Malamulo, villagers asked him to start a school. Mark Chakachadza started a school and as he taught his eager students the "Three Rs," most likely under a tree, he used the opportunity to bring the Adventist message to them. When Malamulo Mission School opened for classes at the start of 1907, Mark Chakachadza went to the mission not to continue his education but to present the request of the people of his village.

Cyrus J. Rogers, the new director of Malamulo mission from January 1907, was impressed when he heard of the work of Mark Chakachadza. On his trip to Malamulo, Chakachadza went with a group of people whom he had converted through his evangelical work in his village. Whether this was a ploy to influence the opinion of the Adventist missionary at Malamulo to favourably consider the request, is not known from the scanty sources available. What is certain, however, is that Chakachadza's trip to Malamulo was a success because all the 18 Bible class students, whom he had thoroughly instructed in the teaching of the SDA church, were baptized.[17]

Perhaps the greatest success of the trip to Malamulo was Rogers' willingness to help the people of Chakulemeka. Although Rogers readily agreed to honour the request, he was apprehensive to come to an area that, following an initial inquiry, was thought to be the religious sphere of other Christian organizations. In 1913, in a speech to the special sitting

---

[16] EWEP "History of SEAU," p. 7.
[17] See *General Conference Bulletin*, vol. 3, 1913 no. 16, p. 252.

of the GC, Rogers gave the reason for this apprehensiveness. He told those present that

> We had a great problem on hand as to how we would get along where the other missions occupy the field. One of the boys from our school went home and was asked by the villagers to open a school off one hundred and fifty (sic) miles from Malamulo mission. He opened the school and began work ... He came to our mission and wanted us to support him but we said, "we cannot do that because you are in the territory of another mission."... Now there is an organized church there, sixteen native schools and about twenty teachers at work - all in four years.[18]

Rogers' fear of possible intrusion into areas claimed by other missions was not baseless. By the turn of the twentieth century, several Christian missions had opened their work in the Central Shire, a wide area that comprised the modern districts of Blantyre (including Matope), Neno and Chikwawa. The Dutch Reformed Church (DRC), Zambezi Industrial Mission (ZIM), Watch Tower Movement (WTM), Church of Scotland (CS) and the Montfortian Fathers (RC) were scattered in and around this wide area.[19] It should be noted that the Adventist church was not the first Christian mission in the Neno area. In 1906, two years before Adventists established their mission, the RC through the Montfort Fathers had already opened a mission called St. Armand in Neno. Later, the Montfort Fathers at St. Armand opened over twenty out-schools in the area and boasted a total enrollment of six hundred and seventy two students.[20]

Out-schools like these, scattered further away from the main mission, were the basis of conflicts among missionary societies over adherents and territory in the early years of missionary penetration in Malawi. For example, due to a conflict that developed between the Missionaries of Africa (RC) and the DRC in Lilongwe in 1911, the government decided to

---

[18] Ibid.

[19] For aspects of Christian missions in Central Shire, see MNA District Commissioner's Notes, Neno (Central Shire District), 1 March 1907-1931 March 1950.

[20] Hubert Reijnaerts, Ann Nielsen and Matthew Schoffeleers, *Montfortians: Their Spirituality and Pastoral Approach*, Blantyre: CLAIM-Kachere, 1997, p. 80.

impose a two-mile limit between schools, so that "after 1912 the tape measure became an indispensable piece of evangelist's equipment, and the sight of priests intrepidly pacing their way through thick bush was not uncommon."[21] It is likely that this was the kind of "conflict" Rogers was referring to when he was apprehensive to come to the Matandani area to start Adventist work.

Another problem seems to have been that Rogers did not want to open another mission so close to Malamulo. In fact, when he asked the GC for missionaries, it was his intention to send them to start Adventist work in northern Malawi. There were other problems too that Rogers had to take care of first before he could undertake other responsibilities. In spite of his dedication and pioneering work in the establishment of SDA work in Malawi, Thomas Branch left a much weaker mission at Malamulo when he returned to America in 1907. The quarrels with his co-founder, Joseph Booth, in the running of the mission, did not go unnoticed by the government and other missionary societies in the country. Harry Langworthy has stated that "although Branch had been a loyal adherent to Adventist beliefs and practices, his leadership had been uninspired, unimaginative, cautious and in some ways, not very competent."[22]

Further, Rogers was trying to clear the Adventist name that had been wrongly linked to the entry of Ethiopianism in Malawi.[23] This was mainly because of the church's association with Joseph Booth and the fact that Thomas Branch, a black person, had been in charge of its mission. One reason that led to the replacement of Branch was the fact that the Adventist church at the time feared that keeping Branch (a black person and an American) as head of its work at a time when the church was under suspicion after its founder, Booth, had been deported because of

---

[21] Ibid., pp. 136-137.

[22] Langworthy, *Life of Joseph Booth*, p. 430.

[23] According to George Shepperson and Thomas Price, etymologically, the term "Ethiopianism" had its origins from Biblical texts such as Psalm 31:86, "Ethiopia shall soon stretch out her hands to God." The movement that became synonymous with Black Nationalism started in South Africa in the 1870s when black people, stung by colour prejudices, set up their own churches instead of continuing to bear the humiliation of segregation in white churches. The John Chilembwe Rising of 1915 in Malawi has been suggested to have a strong Ethiopian background. See *Independent African*, pp. 72-73.

his pro-Ethiopian activities would "lend support to the idea that Adventists did perhaps after all, believe and practice the beliefs of Africa for Africans [of Booth]."[24] Therefore, by removing Branch the church was trying to win back the trust of the government.

It is also probable that the removal of Branch was a step in the direction of attempts by the church to establish a working relationship with other churches, something that Branch had refused to do.[25] During the time Branch was director at Malamulo, he had refused all offers of friendship from other churches, a fact that led other churches to confirm the suspicion that the Adventist church was bent at undermining other churches. What mostly worried other churches was Branch's refusal to join the Council of Missions whose interest was to demarcate areas of influence. Branch's attitude was probably influenced by the fact he had "little in common with those churches or because his being black could have proven embarrassing to the European council members of the Council of Missions in Malawi."[26] It is likely that Branch's attitude was reinforced by the fact the SDA church does not practice ecumenism.[27]

Towards the end of 1907 Rogers, travelling by *machila* (portable hammock carried by porters), came to Chakulemeka village; first, as an acknowledgement of the evangelical work of Mark Chakachadza and second, to assess if it was possible to set up a mission school as the people of the village had requested earlier in the year. However, not

---

[24] Langworthy, *Life of Joseph Booth*, p. 430.

[25] EWEP "History of SEAU," pp. 8-9. See also Bilima ,"The SDA in Malawi," p. 36.

[26] EWEP "History of SEAU," pp. 8-9.

[27] Richard W. Schwarz has outlined seven reasons why Adventists are opposed to ecumenism. (I) the interpretation of the Genesis stories of creation and the flood in a literal or figurative way, (2) the view of God as One who might periodically choose to break into human history in a miraculous way, (3) faith in a social-gospel type of reformation of mankind, (4) the Sabbath, its origin, purpose and perpetuity, (5) the nature of man and his state in death, (6) the imminence and prime importance of the second advent of Christ and (7) Adventist emphasis on prophecy including the conviction that Adventists were prophetically portrayed in Revelation 14 as having a commission to call God's people into a special reformatory work at the end of time. See Richard W. Schwarz, *Light Bearers to the Remnant*, California: Pacific Press, 1979, p. 540. See also, Klaus Fiedler, "The 'Smaller' Churches and 'Big' Government," in Matembo S. Nzunda and Kenneth R. Ross, *Church, Law and Political Transition in Malawi 1992-94*, Gweru: Mambo, 1995, pp. 166-168.

everyone in the area welcomed Rogers' visit. Upon hearing that a missionary had arrived in the area, some village headmen adjacent to Chakulemeka village became suspicious and resentful. These wrongly feared that the missionary had come with the intention of taking over their land.

It is likely that Rogers could have returned to Malamulo without fulfilling the wishes of headman Chakachadza and his people if a "miraculous" coincidence had not happened. This was the news that a nearby estate called Banga, situated close to Chakulemeka village, was about to be sold due to financial problems. Before he left for Malamulo mission, Rogers made inquiries about the estate, especially one of the estate's farms called Matandani. After an initial survey of Matandani farm, Rogers was convinced that the farm was suitable for a mission. The idea of a farm alongside evangelical work was one of the prerequisites in the selection of an area for a mission not only for Adventists, but also for other early missionary societies in Malawi. These farms provided land for growing crops and raising animals both for sale and for food. The produce from the farms was particularly important in providing food to the growing missionary and African communities of the missions. Farming also enabled students to get hands on experience of the agricultural skills that many of the missions taught. Malamulo mission for example, was purchased because it had over 2000 acres of farmland. Matandani farm, with 216 acres of land, was equally attractive for similar reasons.

Rogers had other reasons for liking Matandani farm. With a cool mountain climate encouraged by the Kirk Range, he concluded that the place was suitable for European settlement. For him, the area was "much more healthful than at Malamulo."[28] As the superintendent of Adventist work in Malawi, Rogers did not waste time in making inquiries with the intention of purchasing this estate when he returned to Malamulo. On 9 December 1907, Matandani became an SDA property

---

[28] EWEP Virgil E. Robinson, "Third Angel Over Africa," (typescript), p. 181.

when a sum of 40 pounds was paid to the trustees of the bankrupt Banga Estate.[29]

William Frederick Goodison was the proprietor of Banga Estate. A number of cash crops were grown and these included tobacco, cotton, rubber, coffee, and pepper. Goodison is infamous for a shortness of temper that usually resulted in the beating, with a cane, of his workers whom he suspected of slacking in their farm work. The caning earned him a nickname, *Kachipande* (the caner). Payment for work at the estate was mainly in kind. Pieces of cloth and salt were the common forms of payment.[30]

In general, Banga estate was not a success and by the start of 1907, it was facing bankruptcy. On 5 November 1907, the estate of W.F. Goodison was "adjudged bankrupt" by the High Court of Malawi.[31] Rogers was pleased with the acquisition of Matandani farm that "when calling for new workers, it had been the intention of Elder Rogers that they would take over the direction of Malamulo while he and his wife proceeded to pioneer work in Angoniland."[32] The call for workers for the unreached hinterland of Malawi was heeded in 1908 when an American couple, Samuel and Ruth Konigmacher, arrived.

Establishment of Matandani Mission, 1908-1914

The establishment of Matandani mission is usually credited to the pioneering work of Samuel M. Konigmacher, the director of the maiden mission and Peter Nyambo, his African assistant.[33] Konigmacher (1877-

---

[29] MiP Deed of Sale between the Registrar of the High Court, Blantyre and Joel Cyrus Rogers of Seventh-day Adventists, 19 December 1907, courtesy of Matandani Mission Secondary School Administration. See also MNA District Commissioner's Notes, Neno (Central Shire) District Book, Volume II, 1923-1928, 1 April to 31 March.

[30] Interview, Matsimbe, S. Kaphale and E. Kaphale.

[31] MiP Deed of Sale.

[32] EWEP Robinson, "Third Angel," p. 182.

[33] Langworthy, *Life of Joseph Booth,* p. 431.

1952),[34] a second-generation Seventh-day Adventist, attended Battle Creek Sanitarium in Michigan, USA, then the most famous Adventist Health College and Seminary, where most of the missionaries to foreign missions trained. At Battle Creek Sanitarium, the famous Dr. J.H. Kellogg[35] (whose father, J.P. Kellogg was the founder member of the Western Reform Institute before it became Battle Creek Sanitarium) and others taught courses in alternative diets, hydrotherapy and electric therapies.[36] The emphasis of the sanitarium was on natural remedies as the cure of many illnesses. This health reform became a very important aspect of Adventist teaching.[37]

Konigmacher married Ruth Mason, also a trained nurse from Battle Creek Sanitarium. Ruth and Samuel Konigmacher arrived in Malawi at the beginning of 1908 through the kindness of Ruth's father who paid for their sea fare from America to Africa. After a couple of months at Malamulo mission where they stayed for their orientation, they were sent to pioneer work at Matandani. The Konigmachers had three children, all boys: Samuel Martin, James and Arthur Earle. After leaving Malawi, Konigmacher worked at Rusangu mission in Zambia. In 1916, he pioneered in the establishment of Musofa mission, located just outside

---

[34] The biographical information on the early life of S.M. Konigmacher was made available to me by Konigmacher's great niece, Sandra Konigmacher, through e-mail between September 1998 and April 1999. Sandra Konigmacher lives in Washington DC, USA.

[35] Today, J.H. Kellogg is better remembered for the Kellogg's brand of breakfast foods that he founded. For aspects of J.H. Kellogg, see Richard Schwarz, "John Harvey Kellogg: An American Reformer," Ph.D. dissertation, University of Michigan, USA, 1964. Dr. Kellogg clashed with the church leadership mainly over his promotion of pantheistic ideas about the presence of God, clearly against Adventist doctrines (i.e. the immanence of God in all living creatures). Another serious clash with the church was over the control of the Battle Creek Sanitarium of which he was in charge. He was subsequently dropped from SDA church membership on 10 November 1907. See Jeff Reich, "A.T. Jones and the Church," *Our Firm Foundation*, vol. 7, no. 11, pp. 4-7. For some aspects of the Kellogg problem see also Schwarz, *Light Bearers*, pp. 282-298.

[36] Sandra Konigmacher says that a novel written about the health reforms of the time titled "The Road to Wellville," describes health programs as "a satire fitness craze, a kind of everything old is new again type." (Sandra Konigmacher, e-mail communication).

[37] For aspects of the Adventist health reform see Schwarz, *Light Bearers*, pp. 104-116 and 598-614. For aspects of church's teaching on health, see, Ellen G. White, *Ministry of Healing*, Mountain View, California: Pacific Press, 1913.

the Congo (today the Democratic Republic of Congo) border.[38] About 1932, Ruth died at Lirimba Hill Mission in Kalabo, Zambia where she and her husband had been missionaries probably after leaving Musofa. Samuel Konigmacher wrote a popular Adventist booklet titled, "In the Lion Country." According to Sandra Konigmacher, when it came time to retire and return to the States, Samuel Konigmacher reluctantly returned to America, a country he described as "that sin country." He however retired to Honolulu where in old age he continued to do some SDA activities. It is alleged that one day towards the end of 1952 Konigmacher went insane. After that, he was confined to his room until his death on 11 November 1952.

As there were no funds to purchase a new site in northern Malawi, Rogers sent Samuel Konigmacher to develop the new station at Matandani. Konigmacher, Nyambo and their families arrived at Matandani in the middle of 1908 and soon the difficult work of setting up a mission began. Besides Morrison Malinki, Peter Nyambo was the most important and influential Adventist African worker in the early years of the church in Malawi. In fact, Nyambo's own story requires a separate treatment but only those elements of it may be mentioned here which concern his activities up to and at Matandani mission.[39]

Born in about 1884, Peter Nyambo, a Ngoni from Ntcheu district, enrolled at the Scottish Mission School in Blantyre in 1897 where he stayed for five years. Nyambo came under the influence of Booth when the two met while Nyambo was at Blantyre mission. A relationship was immediately struck and like Chilembwe, Booth took Nyambo outside the

---

[38] Arthur W. Spalding, *Origin and History of Seventh-day Adventists*, volume 4, Washington: Review and Herald Publishing Association, 1962, p. 22.

[39] The story of Nyambo requires an appraisal. His work as an Adventist worker, his separation with the Adventists in 1911, his work in East Africa, his association with Booth and its ramifications, his document "The Rhodesia-Nyasaland Appeal" and petition to the King of England, his stay and education in England, his travels in Europe, his work and stay in South Africa for over thirty years, his work at Malamulo and Matandani missions and his independent church in Ntcheu are some of the issues that needs to be appraised. For aspects concerning the discussion in this section, see Langworthy, *Life of Joseph Booth*, pp. 427-439. See also Shepperson and Price, *Independent African*, pp. 203-209.

confines of Africa,[40] this time not to America as in the case of Chilembwe but to Great Britain, an experience that was to have profound influence on Nyambo. As noted earlier, Booth was at Malamulo by 1902 and as was his habit, convinced his friends and students at his former missions to follow him. Nyambo came to Malamulo for this reason and a year later when Booth left Malawi he took with him the young Nyambo to Britain.

In 1904 while in Britain, Nyambo temporarily parted ways with Booth not because of any quarrels between the two, but because Booth did not have the finances to keep him and pay for his school fees. This was a repeat situation to that of Chilembwe. Booth had taken Chilembwe to America in 1897 but the two parted ways because Booth did not have the finance to continue supporting him. In Britain, Booth, who until this time was still a paid Adventist worker, managed to find some sympathetic Adventists willing to support Nyambo.[41] This was the first time that Adventists in Europe had direct contact with an African connected with their first mission in Central Africa and in need of local workers and converts. In Nyambo, the Adventists saw an opportunity to expand their influence in Africa, and for this reason they did not hesitate to accept the responsibility of taking care of Nyambo. The Adventists enrolled Nyambo at their school, Dumcombe Hall, in 1904 and it was while he was at this school that the Adventists baptized Nyambo into their church.

Nyambo visited much of Great Britain and some European countries such as Germany, Holland, Belgium, the Mediterranean countries and Switzerland, places where he addressed many Adventist gatherings. In fact, Nyambo himself claimed that for four months between 1904 and 1905 he spoke at 160 Adventist meetings.[42] It was in Britain where he was employed as a full-time worker of the Adventist church. In 1906, as had been planned for him by the church in Britain, Nyambo was sent as a missionary back to Africa. First, he was sent to Tanzania where he joined the missionary, A.C. Enns as his assistant.[43] Later, with missionary

---

[40] Some aspects of Chilembwe and the 1915 Rising are the focus of the next section.

[41] Booth officially broke ties with the SDA church in 1906, three years after he had left Malamulo mission. See Langworthy, *Life of Joseph Booth*, p. 148.

[42] Langworthy, *Life of Joseph Booth*, p. 429.

[43] Stefan Höschele, a University of Malawi PhD candidate, is currently working on this history.

A.G. Carscallen, Nyambo was sent to co-pioneer Adventist work in Kenya, establishing an Adventist station at a place called Gendia near Kisumu. In December 1907, Nyambo returned to Malawi where he joined Malamulo Mission School as both teacher and missionary assistant to C.J. Rogers. When Konigmacher arrived at the beginning of 1908, he found Nyambo at Malamulo.

As noted earlier, Konigmacher and Nyambo were sent to pioneer Adventist work at Matandani mission. The two chose a hilly site across the Matandani River in Traditional Authority Dambe's area. There, a wattle and daub church and living quarters were constructed. The new station was named Matandani either after the nearby river or after the name of the farm. Fulfilling the wishes of the people in the area, a school under the general supervision of Malamulo mission was begun. The little church served as classroom. The earliest classes were class A and B and met alternatively in the little mud church. Konigmacher, his wife Ruth and Peter Nyambo were both evangelists and teachers of this new community and its surrounding areas. The success of this pioneering work was evident by the fact that by the end of 1908, about eleven people were converted in and around the new mission.[44]

One person in the group of the first converts was Moses Chauluka, who before the Adventist missionaries came to the area was a slave-hunter and warrior. After his conversion and probably due to his zeal in evangelical work and assistance to Konigmacher and Nyambo at the mission, he was sent to Malamulo for some evangelical training where he stayed for a few months. Upon his return, he worked as an evangelist in the Matandani mission area. The few sources about him suggest that Chauluka worked in the Matandani area until around the time of World War I.[45] Sometime towards the end of the middle of 1908, Philip Chinyama joined Konigmacher and Nyambo at Matandani mission. Although details of Chinyama's work at the mission are generally unavailable (as is the case with many African workers), his stay at the

---

[44] See Bilima, "The SDA in Malawi," p. 41.

[45] See, Matandani Secondary School prospectus, 1998 (unpublished), interview F.L. Matsimbe, Matandani mission, 26 August 1998 and *General Conference Bulletin*, vol. 3, 1913 no. 16, p. 251. It should be noted that further details on Chauluka are obscure.

mission and more so his relationship with Konigmacher and Nyambo, had unintended consequences on the church as regards the Chilembwe Rising.[46]

Chakachadza's little school at Chakulemeka village continued to operate on the periphery of the mission. Later, it became one among many out-schools that mushroomed around the mission. The earliest students the school at the mission attracted were married. This turned out to be an advantage because at that age most of them knew how to construct traditional living structures. Konigmacher and Nyambo used this skill of the students to construct basic infrastructure at the mission. Students were not required to pay money as school fees but instead paid by working at the mission farm and other areas at the mission. In fact, it was the practice of the SDA church when it started at Malamulo to pay students up to 3/- as a way of attracting them to attend the school. This was stopped when C.J. Rogers came. Instead, students at Malamulo worked on the school farm as part of payment to attend school.[47]

At Matandani mission, Konigmacher followed a similar pattern. Students worked at the farm or constructed structures in the morning and attended classes in the afternoon.[48] Students from outlying areas were allowed to construct temporary living quarters around the infant mission and lived there with their families. As enrollment steadily increased, the barns previously used to store pepper at the farm were transformed into classrooms. In 1910, Elders R.C. Porter and Royce, the former being the superintendent of Adventist work in Southern Africa at the time, visited Malawi. What is significant about that visit to the story of Samuel

---

[46] The details of Chinyama's story as they are relevant to the Matandani mission story are covered in the next section.

[47] EWEP, "History of SEAU," p. 10.

[48] The demand for manual labour from students is one of the fundamental teachings of the Adventist church. Based on Genesis 2:15, the church teaches that one of the ways to stay healthy is for people to love doing manual work. In this regard, the church encourages its training institutions to adopt a programme where young people are required to do manual work or in Adventist terminology, do "mission work" as part of their training. Ellen White taught that true education is the one that trains a person mentally, physically and spiritually. See Ellen G. White, *Education*, Mountain View, California: Pacific Press, 1952.

Konigmacher is that when they visited Matandani, they ordained Samuel there, making that event the first at the maiden mission.[49]

Progress at the mission was slow but steady and Samuel Konigmacher's fluency in *Chichewa,* a language he learned quickly through the assistance of Nyambo, eased his dealings with his African staff and students. Some of the wattle and daub structures were slowly being replaced with those of burnt bricks. The age of students at the school gradually become younger. By 1911, ten out-schools of Matandani mission were established as more local teachers came from Malamulo and offered assistance to Ruth and Samuel Konigmacher and Peter Nyambo. These schools were Malimba, Mlemeka, Nadzanga, Lumbe, Mwandaza, Akunkhoma, Kalanga, Manguo, Malambo and Nseula.[50] Together, about four hundred students attended these schools.[51] It should be noted that out-schools only offered elementary classes. Students who successfully completed their education at the out-schools were allowed to come to the mission school to do upper classes which went up to standard three. It is worth noting that as per the policy of the church at the time, English was taught only at Malamulo Mission School, the reason given being that English was irrelevant to the needs of Africans.[52]

The full story of Nyambo at Matandani mission is largely unavailable from both written and oral sources. The little information obtainable is that he worked at Matandani mission with Konigmacher until 1911, the year he severed ties with the church.[53] There were two main reasons why Nyambo broke ties with the SDA church. One reason seems to have been the insensitivity of Rogers, then superintendent of Adventist work, in dealing with the concerns of Nyambo. When Nyambo left Kenya in 1908, some of his luggage (mostly books) was left behind with the understanding that the church would transport them to Malawi for him. It

---

[49] EWEP, "History of the SEAU,", p. 16.

[50] MNA District Commissioner's Notes, Neno, Central Shire, 1 January to 31 December 1932, Volume 14.

[51] EWEP Robinson, "Third Angel," p. 184.

[52] Langworthy, *Life of Joseph Booth*, p. 430.

[53] See ibid., p. 431.

would appear that Rogers did not take an interest in making sure that the luggage got to Nyambo on time. Although Rogers did not communicate with Nyambo about the reasons for the delay, the problem seems to have been lack of money. Nyambo and Rogers exchanged correspondence over the issue but not much progress was made - Nyambo accusing the missionary of neglecting his needs and Rogers generally ignoring to explain the reasons for the delay. In desperation, Nyambo went as far as telling the Adventist missionary that he was working very hard at Matandani and yet the church was not showing its appreciation. To support this claim, Nyambo mentioned that out of the ten out-schools the mission had established by 1911, six were founded by him.[54] What seemed to have infuriated Nyambo was the fact that although a missionary eventually brought the books to Malamulo mission from Kenya via South Africa, Rogers neither told Nyambo about it nor send them to Matandani. When Nyambo came to know about it later, the books had been eaten by termites. The other reason is the Joseph Booth factor. During the time Nyambo worked for the Adventist church, there was effective communication between the two. It would appear that Nyambo kept Booth informed of how the Adventists were treating him. It should be noted that by 1911, the year Nyambo's relationship with the church was not very good, Booth was planning to re-enter Malawi and was in need of African workers for his new ventures. Booth continued to send Nyambo Baptist tracts and information about new ventures. Exactly what the two friends said about the Adventist church at this time is not known from the available sources. But perhaps the influence of Booth on the final decision for Nyambo to leave the Adventist church is made clear from the letter that Nyambo wrote to Booth immediately after he left the Adventists in September or October of 1911. Nyambo wrote, "Now what you said; it is quite true, about these people [S.D.A]. Now I am out of their mission; this time I am not going to tell you any things (sic) till I come there if God wills."[55]

Apart from Peter Nyambo, Philip Chinyama and Moses Chauluka so far mentioned, a number of African personnel worked at the mission. Al-

---

[54] Ibid.
[55] Ibid.

though their names and the details of their work are mostly unavailable, it cannot be disputed that these workers contributed to the success of the early work at the mission through both evangelization and teaching. Losson Yendayenda and Moffat Tchona were some of the early teacher-evangelists who worked at the mission and in the surrounding areas. Especially at the out-schools[56] the contribution of these early teacher-evangelists was very pronounced and through them, such schools multiplied around the infant mission. Apart from offering the much-needed education in the surrounding villages, out-schools were used as evangelistic tools. In 1913, S.M. Konigmacher explained this well to a group of Adventist church leaders in America. He said:

> When we find a group of villages, a center, where we think it will warrant a white worker we send to that field a white worker. Then this white worker goes out and finds smaller centers, not large enough to place a white worker and there we place that native evangelist, and we instruct that native evangelist to begin Bible classes and to instruct the natives, in his district in regard to the points of our faith. On Friday and on Sabbath he is instructed to get together the natives in the different villages near by, and preach to them the gospel, to help them, and to lead them to Christ. Some have said to me, is not it awful to be in Africa among all the black people, and not be able to see a white face. But we do not go to that field for complexions, but we go there for souls, and God is giving us souls.[57]

Konigmacher's speech reveals that missionaries as well as local workers were responsible for the establishment of missions like Matandani. One of the missing elements in the history of Adventist missions in Africa has been an acknowledgement of the African contribution in the establishment and development of these missions. A large portion of existing literature consists mainly of missionary endeavours and of little

---

[56] After independence in 1964, church controlled out-schools of all missionary societies were placed under the control of district councils.

[57] MiP General Conference Bulletin, p. 251.

African contribution, creating the impression that early missionaries established missions with little or no local help. A lone missionary or a pair of missionaries, fresh from America or Britain into the wild hinterland of Africa with hardly any knowledge of the local culture and language, if not having superhuman abilities, surely relied on the help of some dedicated local people in the difficult task of establishing missions. It is the author's contention that although information on the early African pioneers is sketchy, they nevertheless contributed substantially as interpreters, guides and as this study shows as teachers, evangelists and even pioneers of missions. As the case of Matandani mission shows, in Konigmacher's speech was an admission that African workers played a substantial role in the pioneering years of the mission.[58]

Samuel and Ruth Konigmacher's missionary work was not without personal sacrifice and loss. In 1909 they lost their first-born son, Samuel-Martin, to malaria, and he became the first white person to be buried at the mission cemetery. Four years later, tragedy struck again when their second child, James, succumbed to illness. He was also buried at the cemetery.[59] Writing about the death of his son James, Konigmacher said:

> He is lying beside his little brother on the hillside across the stream. He died at evening. The boys went and dug the little missionary grave. When they came back, we could not part with him, then laid him on his bed until morning. Then I carried him over myself and one of the teachers put him in his last resting-place.[60]

---

[58] One factor that continues to sideline the African contribution in the pioneering work of the church has been the attitude of African workers and members themselves. For example, during research for this study, the author found out that most of the oral informants gave scanty data of fellow African workers but emphasized the work of missionaries. A case in point is that of F.L. Matsimbe. When the author asked him to detail the missionaries he remembered having worked at the mission, he noted all those he knew and even wrote their details on a piece of paper. When the author asked him to do the same for African workers he said that there wasn't much to write about.

[59] Note that the graves of the two Konigmacher children at Matandani mission cemetery are not clearly marked unlike that of Elsie Annie Davy.

[60] EWEP "History of SEAU," p. 20.

Towards the end of 1911, C.J. Rogers went home to America on furlough. Although he returned in 1914, he did not stay at Malamulo but pioneered Adventist work in southern Tanzania and later in 1920 with a local convert, Joseph N. Hlubi, pioneered SDA work in Swaziland.[61] In the absence of the Rogers, the Konigmachers came to Malamulo until the new missionary for Malamulo, C.J. Robinson, a British national, arrived at the close of 1911.[62] The Konigmachers returned to Matandani where they stayed until 1913, the same year they went on furlough. They returned at the beginning of 1914 but stayed only for a while at Matandani. Their interest now lay in opening up work among the Ngoni people of Mozambique. The governor-general of Maputo, then called Lorenço Marques, rejected their visa application to enter Mozambique. Instead, the Konigmachers were sent as missionaries to Zambia.[63]

The personal life of Samuel Konigmacher exemplifies the tragedy that befell many early missionaries to Africa. By the time that he returned to the States on retirement, Konigmacher was already a heartbroken man. Two of his children did not survive him since they succumbed to a tropical illness. His only surviving son, Arthur Earle, refused to go to America with him. According to available sources, Arthur stayed behind in Africa where he joined the British army during World War II. After that he was never heard of again except a rumour that has remained with his extended family in America and Germany that Arthur married an African woman somewhere in Zimbabwe where he made his home.[64] The greatest blow to Konigmacher was surely the death of his wife in Zambia, herself another example of the sacrifices that many missionaries made for the evangelization of Africa. In all, Konigmacher had lost all his immediate family by the time he returned to the States. It is small wonder that he went insane before his death in 1952.

---

[61] *Seventh-day Adventist Encyclopedia*, 1976 "Swaziland" quoted in Stephen Jacobs Masusku, "New Approaches for Seventh-day Adventists in Swaziland," DMin, Andrews University, USA, 1996, p. 61.

[62] EWEP Robinson, "Third Angel," p. 186.

[63] Ibid., p. 188-189.

[64] Sandra Konigmacher is convinced that Arthur Earle born in 1910 at Matandani mission, if still living, resides somewhere in Africa. Ibid., e-mail communication.

The seven years of the Konigmachers at Matandani mission were largely foundational. Their stay at the mission, apart from their pioneering work and that of Nyambo could have gone down quietly into the pages of the history of Adventists in Malawi had it not been for the John Chilembwe Rising of 1915. Among other factors, the government alleged that the Adventist church, through the activities of Konigmacher at Matandani mission and Nyambo's association with Booth, was involved in the Rising.

Impact of the Chilembwe Rising of 1915

In 1915, John Chilembwe, a Malawian Baptist minister of the American National Baptist Convention, Inc., of the Providence Industrial Mission in Chiradzulu district and a protégé of Booth, led an abortive rebellion against the colonial government.[65] The prime nondescript[66] mission suspected in complicity in the Rising was the Adventist church and on the surface, justifiably so; for Joseph Booth, John Chilembwe and Peter Nyambo, had close associations with Morrison Malinki[67] and the Adventist church. Although in general most of the nondescript missions were under suspicion for complexity in the Rising; the Adventist church was one of the prime suspects in this complicity. For Adventists, the year 1915 was particularly a bad one because it was the year that the church was in mourning following the death of its spiritual leader, Ellen G. White, who died on 12 February 1915.[68]

George Shepperson and Thomas Price mention that rumours circulating in Malawi soon after the Rising, made worse by an article that appeared in the *Nyasaland Times* of 11 February 1915, indicated that whether directly or indirectly, the Adventist church had a hand in the affair. C.J. Robinson, at the time the superintendent of Adventist work in

---

[65] For his life, see: George Shepperson and Tom Price, *Independent African. John Chilembwe and the Nyasaland Rising of 1915*, Blantyre: CLAIM-Kachere, ⁶2000 (Edinburgh 1958).

[66] A description coined by the *Nyasaland Times* in 1915 to describe smaller missions that were thought to promote Ethiopianism (i.e. African Nationalism) and through their teachings were believed to "unsettle the native mind".

[67] Morrison Malinki's alleged link to the Rising is fully discussed in the next chapter.

[68] Schwarz, *Light Bearers*, p. 414.

the country and stationed at Malamulo mission, wrote a letter of refutation to this spate of allegations to the editor of the *Nyasaland Times*.[69] In the editorial of September 1915, the *Nyasaland Times* acknowledged receipt of the letter and made sneering comments on it but never published Robinson's letter. The editorial stated that:

> the grounds on which we criticize the Malamulo mission are similar. While their intentions may be excellent, the practical outcome of their work is to unsettle the natives and to bring chaos into the native religious world. To speak very plainly, we think that hair splitting over the observance of Sunday is calculated to do immense harm to the natives and we go further and say that the government would be well advised to stop all such propaganda. It may be said that this is an interference with the liberty of the subject but so is all that the government does and this doctrine of interference with liberty of the subject has to be controlled by the higher doctrine of the well being of the whole community. Not only so but government has already affirmed the principle that where any propaganda is likely to lead to breaches of public peace the government can forbid such propaganda.[70]

Such uncompromising response by a government-controlled press was tantamount to a direct accusation that the church was in no way innocent of the events that unfolded in the country in 1915. Notwithstanding these allegations, it was later proven that the Adventist church had no hand in the Chilembwe Rising of 1915. In fact, the 1916 Commission of Inquiry into the troubles in Malawi found the church free from all allegations. Although the appellation "Adventist" continued to be a vague term of suspicion, the church was left alone to conduct its affairs without interference.[71]

---

[69] Shepperson and Price, *Independent African*, p. 328.

[70] *Nyasaland Times* editor's original manuscript, see MNA File No. S6/SDB/1/12/.

[71] See Shepperson and Price, *Independent African*, p. 329-330.

There is a question however that should be asked about this issue. If the SDA church was not "involved" in the Rising why did the civil authorities suspect the church in the first place? In this suspicion, what part did Matandani mission contribute to these allegations? Several reasons attempt to explain this. The association that the Adventist church through Samuel Konigmacher had with Philip Chinyama was one reason for these allegations. Chinyama and an associate Philemon Kadamanja both from Ntcheu district attended Malamulo Mission School from 1903 to 1908. The two did not find Joseph Booth at Malamulo in 1903 for he had just left either voluntarily or by government order because of his pro-Ethiopian views. The two however found Peter Nyambo, a protégé of Booth also from Ntcheu district, just before Nyambo left for South Africa where Booth was waiting for him for their trip to Britain. It is likely that Nyambo introduced them to the views of Booth.[72] Chinyama remained at Malamulo until early 1908, the same year the Konigmachers arrived at Malamulo at the start of their missionary work in Africa.

When Konigmacher and Nyambo established a mission school at Matandani as earlier noted, Chinyama was one of the early African teachers to come and work there. It should be noted that Mark Chakachadza, a schoolmate at Malamulo mission in the years up to 1906 and even Nyambo himself, as the assistant to Konigmacher and in need of workers, likely influenced Chinyama's decision to work at Matandani mission. Chinyama's stay at Matandani was brief. In late 1908, barely a year at Matandani mission, he joined another mission, the Church of Christ, who baptized him into their fellowship. In 1909, he moved again and this time joined the Nyasa Industrial Mission at Ntambanyama in Thyolo where, again, he stayed for a short time. About 1910 he left for Bulawayo, Zimbabwe and a year later he returned. Upon his return, he went to his home area in Ntcheu where he established an independent Baptist type Church of Christ at Dzunje.[73] Up until the time of the Rising, Chinyama was running an independent school besides his small

---

[72] Langworthy, *Life of Joseph Booth*, pp. 391-392.

[73] Ibid., p. 392. See also MNA File no. S42/1/2/1 titled "Seventh-day Baptists or SDB Church of Christ."

congregation. Although he was independent, the Adventist influence on him was still visible for he observed Saturday as the Sabbath in his church.[74] In 1914, he accepted Chilembwe's request to lead a supplementary Rising in the Ntcheu area and for his part in the affair, the government charged him for treason and he was executed in 1915.[75]

Konigmacher and Chinyama established a lasting relationship through their meeting at both Malamulo and Matandani missions. Their relationship continued until 1914 when Konigmacher left Malawi, a year before the Rising. The two had visited each other between 1911 and 1914, Ntcheu and Matandani being a day's walk apart.[76] More significantly, Konigmacher and Chinyama exchanged correspondence regularly as evidenced by the letters that were found by government investigators soon after the Rising. According to Shepperson and Price "the greatest causes for suspicion of him (Konigmacher) however were that he was known to have been friendly at one time with Philip Chinyama and to have had some correspondence with him and to have taken an interest in Chinyama's career as a preacher."[77]

More damaging was news that after the supplementary Rising aborted some of Chinyama's men were seen running towards the direction of Matandani mission probably "as a friendly place from which to escape from the wrath of the government."[78] Although there is no evidence to suggest that Matandani mission harboured Chinyama's men, such a rumour at such a volatile time was sure to cause strong suspicion against the Adventist church. It should be noted that the government was at this time frantically trying to find those who had, directly or indirectly, aided Chilembwe.

---

[74] Shepperson and Price, *Independent African*, p. 248.

[75] MNA File number S42/1/2/1.

[76] All persons interviewed confirmed the possibility of walking the distance. Most of them have actually walked between the two places on a number of occasions.

[77] Shepperson and Price, *Independent African*, p. 328, see also page 466.

[78] Ibid., p. 282. If this allegation is true, the rebels were going to the Kirk Range Mountain caves near Matandani mission. These caves are ideal for hiding because of the thick bush around. When the Ngoni invaded the area in the 1860s, oral accounts suggest that many people hid in these caves. S.J. Kaphale supplied the oral information about the caves. Interview, Matandani mission, 25 August 1998.

In assessing Konigmacher, Shepperson and Price cite other issues about him that may have contributed to the allegations. Konigmacher's German sounding name[79] was enough to cause concern. German-Americans were thought to be behind the delay of America in joining the Allies against Germany in the 1914-1918 World War I. Further, the government had observed that "in the past Konigmacher had difficulties with government over the opening of mission schools and while engaged in an evangelistic campaign in Portuguese Angoniland, close to the Nyasa border, had been accused of upsetting the minds of native Christians."[80]

The problem arose when sometime towards the end of 1912 and during the long school holidays, the ninety or so students of the mission went to their various homes with an Adventist tract promoting the appropriateness of the Sabbath as the biblically warranted day of worship. This tract was written by C.J. Robinson, the new superintendent of Adventist work in Malawi from 1911 to 1920 and stationed at Malamulo. These students distributed the tracts wherever they went. In reference to this incident, Konigmacher says that

> One of my best evangelists went through all the Neno area distributing these tracts. I said to him: "I do not want you to enter into any argument, or get into any trouble. I simply want you to leave the tract with those who can read and the tract will be its own witness." He did this. He went up into our mission boarders, very near to territory that is occupied by the Dutch Reformed Mission. Three of their teachers came out and said to him: "We do not want you to circulate these tracts in our district. If you do, all our boys will leave our schools, and go to your schools." They realize the truth of God when it is presented. We ought at the present time to press up into this unoccupied territory.[81]

---

[79] Königmacher, German for Kingmaker.
[80] Shepperson and Price, *Independent African*, p. 328.
[81] Ibid., MiP General Conference Bulletin, p. 251.

It were reports like these that made it very difficult at the time for the Adventist church to fully convince the government, and most established churches for that matter, that Adventist intentions were good. It should be noted that established churches in Malawi at the time had most government support unlike nondescript churches like the SDA. Worse for the Adventist church, its non-ecumenical stand was viewed with scorn by most established churches and more so with suspicion by the government.

It should also be noted that although Nyambo was not an Adventist by 1915, his earlier association with the church as a worker was a factor to these allegations. Nyambo, who had worked at both Malamulo and Matandani missions had authored, with the support of Joseph Booth, a pamphlet called "The Rhodesia-Nyasaland Appeal" of May 1914. This document was critical of British rule in Central Africa and at one point, the document was thought to be directly responsible for the Rising by British authorities in Malawi. In fact, by the time of the Rising, the document was freely available in Malawi, having been circulated by people like Philip Chinyama.[82]

In conclusion, it is evident that the church's "involvement" in the Rising was no more than a case of guilty-by-association. It would appear that the church's "involvement" was in no way a result of any deliberate effort by the church to be involved in an affair whose outcome and the suspicions it engendered, was greatly regretted by the church.

---

[82] See Langworthy, *Life of Joseph Booth*, p. 433-439.

Chapter 2

REGULAR MISSION WORK 1915-1939

Second Wave of Missionary and National Workers, 1915-1939

The years between 1915 and 1939 saw a steady flow of missionaries who worked at Matandani mission. Some of these stayed briefly while others stayed much longer. In one sense, this period can be described as one of "missionary camping" because in less than twenty years, five missionaries made their presence as directors. This period was also one that saw a steady flow of African workers, some of who served as temporary directors when a missionary director was absent or on his way.

Since the departure of Samuel M. Konigmacher in 1914, a missionary replacement for him was difficult to find. Work at the mission however continued in spite of this. The church did not officially appoint any African worker there to co-ordinate the work. C.J. Robinson supervised Matandani mission from Malamulo. Although no single African worker can be credited to have been particularly involved with administrative work, African teachers at the mission dedicated themselves to teaching and evangelical work both at the main mission and in the outlying areas. This situation continued until towards the end of 1915 when a British couple, H.J. Hurlow[1] and his wife, both trained nurses, came to Malawi to

---

[1] Not to be confused with his brother W.H. Hurlow who went to Malamulo mission to help in the medical work in 1914 and left towards the end of 1915 after contracting bilharzia, a less known and feared disease in those days.

take over the directorship of Matandani. In 1917, at the height of World War I, Hurlow was called up for military service and was attached to the medical corps and sent to Tanzania to fight against the Germans. As he joined the British forces in Tanzania, Hurlow's wife went to Malamulo and took over some medical work that had been left unattended to since the departure of the hydrotherapist,[2] Irene Fourie.[3]

By the time of World War I, Adventist attitude on its members taking up arms had softened. During the American Civil War (1861-1865), the church condemned war and forbade its members taking up arms. Basing its argument on Revelation 6:12-17 and Revelation 13, the church understood war to be the work of the beast (i.e. the forces of evil against God's people), identified by the number 666, that would eventually rule the world and demand that all people worship it or face persecution and death. Again, for Adventists the war situation would not allow them to keep the fourth and sixth commandments (keep the Sabbath holy and do not kill, respectively). However, debate between pacifists and those advocating for active participation in the war raged on in the church. In 1862, the church, as is the policy today, adopted a compromise position. Adventists could be drafted but could not take up arms. Most Adventists upon joining the army took non-combatant roles like joining the medical corps.[4]

During the absence of Hurlow, no missionary was sent to Matandani. Morrison Malinki[5] and Moses Chauluka who were already at Matandani worked briefly as temporary co-directors, the first Africans in that capacity. Malinki's story is not only significant to Matandani mission but to the alleged complicity in the Chilembwe Rising which has been mentioned in the previous section. A pioneer African Adventist worker,

---

[2] Hydrotherapy was an important aspect of Seventh-day Adventist alternative medical treatment, and it was often used in missionary situations.

[3] EWEP Robinson, "Third Angel", pp. 190-191.

[4] See Schwarz, *Light Bearers*, pp. 98-102.

[5] The historical sketch of Kalinde Malinki in this section is based on the accounts of Jaspine Bilima, "James Malinki of Malawi: Church Leader in Cross-cultural Ministry," A Project Report for the Degree of DMin, Andrews University, 1993, pp. 52-65. See also Kalinde's autobiography, MiP "The History of Pastor K.M. Malinki".

Malinki attended Blantyre mission where he trained as a teacher. In 1892 Joseph Booth met and convinced him to teach at Booth's Zambezi Industrial Mission school at Mitsidi. It was at Mitsidi where Malinki met Chilembwe and a relationship between the two developed. Booth baptized Malinki into the ZIM church, and when Booth and Chilembwe went to America in 1897, Malinki opened his own independent schools on a self-supporting basis at Chileka, Monekera, Khungulu, Malabvi, Kanje and Msomera.

In 1900, Booth was back from America and together with Malinki took a contract with the African Lakes Corporation (ALC). Malinki's specific duty was to supervise *mtengatenga* (carriers/porters of goods) from Chikwawa to Blantyre. Malinki did this job until 1901. When Booth founded Malamulo mission he asked Malinki to join him but at that time Malinki was not ready. In 1904, a year after Booth left Malamulo, Thomas Branch finally managed to convince Malinki to join him at Malamulo where Malinki worked as a translator and teacher but still operating his schools. In 1906, Malinki and his wife Rachel were re-baptized[6] into the Adventist church.[7]

To help ease the workload for Malinki, in 1907 C.J. Rogers, then the Adventist missionary at Malamulo, sent three teachers from Malamulo (James D. Ngaiyaye, Jacob Mnalimanji and Izeki R. Mphatsa) to run his schools. Later Rogers asked Malinki to amalgamate his schools with the SDA out-schools. Malinki agreed and subsequently the Adventist church appointed him as inspector of Adventist schools in southern Malawi, a post he held for 13 years. During the organization of the Rising,

---

[6] Re-baptism, i.e. baptizing an already baptized person, is a common practice in the SDA church. Although in some circumstances the church recognizes the baptisms of other churches and accepts people coming into the church from those churches on what is called "profession of faith," the church insists that only its baptism is valid. For aspects of conditions for re-baptism in the church see Yonah H. Matemba, "The Practice of Rebaptism in the Seventh-day Adventist Church," University of Malawi, Department of Theology and Religious Studies, MA module presented at the post-graduate colloquium, Nantipwiri Pastoral Centre, May 1997.

[7] The first baptism at Malamulo mission and indeed in the SDA church in Malawi, took place on 30 September 1905 when seven boys were baptized by Pastor Branch. Out of the group, only two people have been identified. These were the brothers Simon and James Ngaiyaye who later worked for the church. EWEP "History of SEAU," pp. 5-6.

Chilembwe approached his old friend Malinki, with the view to interest him to join the Rising. Malinki politely refused, to the utter disappointment of Chilembwe who called Malinki a coward.

After the Rising, Malinki's association with Booth and Chilembwe was the cause of suspicion by government that the Adventist church was involved in the affair. Two things in the government's eye were the cause for this suspicion. Malinki had signed the African Christian Union memorandum of Joseph Booth, the precursor to Booth's idea of Africa for the Africans.[8] Secondly, when his house was searched, government investigators found correspondence between Malinki and Chilembwe. Malinki was imprisoned for three months at Zomba and spent that time in leg irons. He was however, released after being exonerated from all charges. This exoneration was one of the proofs that the Adventist church did not support the Chilembwe Rising. In about 1917, he was asked to work at Matandani mission as both teacher and pastor and together with Moses Chauluka, Malinki was asked to temporarily manage affairs at the mission until a missionary became available. Apart from his work at the mission, Malinki continued to work as supervisor of Adventist out-schools in southern Malawi.

Hurlow returned to Matandani in 1919 and resumed his position as director. It would appear that the two African leaders did a commendable job during their time as directors. In fact, when Hurlow returned to Matandani he was "greatly encouraged to see the progress that had been made during his absence."[9] Hurlow did not stay long at Matandani because a year after his return he went on furlough and never returned. G.A. Ellingworth who had replaced C.J. Robinson as acting director at Malamulo was asked to head Matandani mission. This was because in 1923 the GC sent A.P. Pond, who was to die tragically, as the new director of Malamulo mission. One Sabbath afternoon in February 1923, Pond, his wife and a few other workers went to have a picnic on the banks of Nsuwadzi River, some four miles away from the mission. They found the river low but when Pond tried to walk along some rocks above

---

[8] For a fuller account of Booth's *Africa for the Africans*, see Laura Perry (ed.), *Joseph Booth: Africa for the Africans*, Blantyre: CLAIM-Kachere, 1996.

[9] EWEP Robinson, "Third Angel," p. 192

the falls, he slipped and fell to his death. He was buried at the little mission cemetery at Malamulo.[10]

For this unfortunate incident, G.A. Ellingworth was called from Matandani to head Malamulo mission until a replacement for Pond was found. Ellingworth stayed at Malamulo until 1925 when, at the formation of the South East Africa Union (SEAU, today called Malawi Union),[11] he was appointed as its first president and his wife as its first secretary-treasurer. The couple moved to Blantyre where the Union office buildings have been ever since. The couple served in those capacities until 1927.[12] The years both Hurlow and Ellingworth stayed at Matandani were largely uneventful. This was to change slightly when the Canadian, W.L. Davy and his wife Elsie Annie arrived at Matandani. The Davys came to the mission in 1923 after spending two years at Malamulo. Davy's immediate impression was that the site where the mission buildings were situated was unsuitable and thus a shift was made to where the mission infrastructure exists today in Traditional Authority Ngozi.[13]

The shift was necessary for a number of reasons. One, crossing the Matandani River from the eastern part of the mission (where the mission farm was located) to the mission buildings was difficult, especially during the rainy season. Two, the old mission site was some distance away from the larger portion of the mission land across the river where the mission farm was. Three, the old mission site was too steep and lacked space for expansion. A church and a primary school were the first structures to be erected on the new mission site. Later, a dispensary and director's house, all made from burnt bricks, were built.[14]

---

[10] No African worker has ever been buried at this cemetery. But when Pastor F. Botomani, the first African President of the Malawi Union died in retirement in August 1998, it is said that the church asked the family to bury him at this cemetery. The family however, preferred to have him buried among his family in Neno, near Matandani mission.

[11] For a detailed account of the origins and development of the Malawi Union, see Bilima, "The SDA in Malawi", pp. 95-96.

[12] EWEP "History of SEAU," pp. 27-28.

[13] The ruins of the first mission site can still be seen today.

[14] Government records of Christian missions in the Neno area indicate that by 1924, Matandani mission had a mission house, a church and a school, all made of brick and exempt from tax.

It was also during this time that the enrollment of single boarding students increased forcing Davy to introduce monetary payment for both tuition and board. The fee for both tuition and board for a term was set at 6/-. Those who could not afford the high fees continued to work at the mission as part of payment. In addition, the school curriculum designed by Konigmacher continued to be followed. The programme was that students generally worked in the morning and attended classes in the afternoon. This was the practice even at Malamulo. It was also during the time of Davy that a goods store was opened at the mission. This was a village store under a storekeeper named Mr. Richie. Basic items like cloths, salt, soap, sugar etc. could now be obtained at the mission.[15]

Table 1: Some Out-Schools Operated by Matandani Mission (c. 1923)[16]

Name of Out-School	Villages Serving
Manguo	Chedanilo, Mpasadala, Chakachadza (sic), Nseula
Lisengwe	Kadambalopa
Mlemeka and Nadzanga	Kalupsya (Mbanga), Chepauchoka, Lumbe (Ziyango)
Nkundi	Danda
Nkulumadzi	Magarata, Mwanduza, Kaperama
Thambani	Kunkhoma, Kanyelamalo, Kalanga, Mpinjiri

Clearly, by 1925 the mission under Davy was slowly turning into a rural metropolitan center. The primary school was now offering up to standard four, a rare development in those days. Students who completed beginning classes at the out-schools continued to come to the mission school to attend the rest of their primary education. Out-schools operated by Matandani mission had been steadily increasing as from the early

---

See MNA District Commissioner's Notes, Neno (Central Shire), District Book, volume III, 1 April 1923-31 March 1928.
[15] Matsimbe, 25 August 1998.
[16] Source: Ibid.

1920s. By 1923, schools like Ngao, Kuyera, Kawaliza and Thinde were added to the existing ten out-schools.[17] This early progress, as evidenced by the proliferation of out-schools shown above, was also achieved because of the dedication of African workers at the mission. Teacher-evangelists from Malamulo Mission School continued to give invaluable help with their services at the mission.[18] Through the efforts of Davy and the African workers at the mission, evangelical work appears to have been bearing fruit at this time. This is evidenced by the building of two prayer houses on the periphery of the mission, at Mitengo and at Kaperano.[19]

The year 1925 began on a tragic note for W.L. Davy. His wife Elsie (1896-1925) fell ill from malaria. As she lay dying, teacher-evangelist Kalulu volunteered to walk all the way to Malamulo mission, some 184 km away, to collect quinine. Sadly, there was no missionary present at Malamulo when he got there and returned in haste to Matandani without the life-saving drug. Kalulu should not have hurried back, for Elsie Annie Davy died as Kalulu made the return journey. She was buried at the mission cemetery on 28 January 1925 beside the Konigmachers' children.[20] After this tragic loss, Davy and his three children went on furlough to their native home in Canada. While there he married Lydia Stickle, a former secretary in Ellen G. White's office. In 1926, Davy and his family returned to Africa but instead of returning to Malawi, he offered to labour in Botswana. Matandani mission remained for a year without a director. At the expiry of his tenure at the Union in 1927, G.A. Ellingworth accepted a call to return to Matandani as director. The Ellingworths' stay at Matandani however, was ephemeral. A year later they accepted

---

[17] MNA District Commissioner's Notes, Neno (Central Shire), District Book, volume II, 20 August 1918-17 January 1923.

[18] MP Matandani School Prospectus, 1998 (draft copy).

[19] MNA District Commissioner's Notes Volume 14, 1 January 1928 to 31 December 1932, Blantyre District Book.

[20] Epitaph for Elsie Annie Davy, Matandani mission cemetery. See also S.G. Maxwell, *I Loved Africa*, January 1975. Photocopied materials courtesy of Pauline Maxwell, Ellen G. White Estate library, Berrien Spring, Michigan, Andrews University, p. 115.

another call to open Adventist work in Tanzania and would work there until 1938.[21]

It is significant to note that by the time the tenure of the Ellingworths at the Union expired, four prominent African pastors were ordained to the ministry.[22] The four pastors were brothers James and Simon Ngaiyaye, Ben Ritch and Albert Kambuwa.[23] In early 1928, Marcus M. Webster came to Matandani as director. Towards the end of the year he made way for the resilient W.L. Davy who returned to head the mission after an absence of three years. Webster went on to head Thekerani mission in southern Thyolo, a mission that had been pioneered by a national worker, Roman Chimera, four years previously.[24] One of the successes of Matandani mission around this time was the establishment of Thambani mission. Situated to the extreme south of Neno in Mwanza district, Thambani mission had started as an out-school of Matandani. In 1928, Thambani School was upgraded to the status of a full mission and a year later Pastor Simon Ngaiyaye went there as its pioneer director.[25]

---

[21] Robinson, "Third Angel", pp. 201-202.

[22] Ordination is such a momentous occasion in the SDA church because it is earned. A pastor may practise for many years but if the church is not satisfied with his devotion to the Adventist church he may never be ordained. Only ordained pastors can, for example, officiate marriages and baptize.

[23] Pastor Albert Kambuwa and two colleagues, D. Nkolokosa and Burton Simon pioneered SDA work among the Yao of Mangochi. So successful were their efforts that in a few years, about 50 people, formerly of the Islamic faith, were converted at three prayer-houses: Makawa, Masika and Jaketi. Pastor Simon Ngaiyaye was sent to Thambani out-school when it was upgraded into an independent mission from Matandani mission as its first director. On his part, Pastor James Ngaiyaye was in 1938 appointed as a Field Secretary of the Malawi Union, the first Malawian Adventist to fill such post. Pastor Ben Ritch was from 1946 the director of Lake View Mission in Central Malawi. See Bilima, "The SDA in Malawi," pp. 42-46.

[24] This mission, thirty-two kilometers from Malamulo mission, was started as an out-school by Mrs. Rogers in 1910 after the local people in the area had asked the SDA missionaries at Malamulo to open a school there. Towards the beginning of the 1920s, Pastor Roman Chimera went to Thekerani where in 1924, under his leadership, as already noted, a mission was established. In 1932, Webster left Thekerani for Munguluni mission in Mozambique ("EWEP History of SEAU," p. 42).

[25] Bilima, "The SDA in Malawi," pp. 42-46.

W.L. Davy's second tenure at Matandani was as eventful as the first. Buildings with burnt bricks continued to replace most of the grass and wattle and daub structures at the mission. Perhaps the most significant evangelical efforts during this period were the annual camp meetings. These annual meetings have a dual purpose: to confirm Adventist members already in the faith to the teachings they hold dear and to serve as a tool of evangelization, targeting non-Adventists. Ideally these meetings are to be held at an area far away from people's homes with the intention of breaking people's daily routines of life so as to allow the Holy Spirit to manifest Himself in the people attending the meetings. In such secluded areas, members pitch a tent or live in temporary shelters for about a week, the period the meetings normally last. The first official camp meeting in the SDA church was held between 1-7 September 1868 on the farm of E.H. Root near Wright. It is recorded that 20,000 people came to hear Ellen White speak. By the end of the meeting, 1,876 people had been converted and were baptized.[26]

In Malawi, the first camp meeting was held at Malamulo from 20 to 28 September 1918. Being the first of its kind in the country, the church's administrators did not put much hope on its success. Pastor Straw from Bulawayo was invited as a guest speaker at this historic meeting. Not leaving anything to chance, the church provided food for those who came to attend the meetings. Adventist believers and would be believers from all corners of the country converged at Malamulo mission. The meeting was such a success because out of 731 attendees, 113 were baptized by the end of that week. From the beginning of the 1920s, changes were made to the organization of the camp meetings.

The provision of free food to attendees was discontinued as a measure to discourage attendance for the sake of succor. It was also financially burdensome to feed so many people. Those coming to the meetings were now required to bring their own food. Consequently, the length of the meetings as it stands today was reduced to a few days to allow people to bring sufficient food to carry them through. Towards the end of the 1920s, the tradition of going to Malamulo mission for the meetings was discontinued and every main mission held its own camp

---

[26] Schwarz, *Light Bearers*, pp. 158-159.

meetings attended by members from churches and prayer-houses under such a mission.[27] This change allowed the other missions and not only Malamulo to develop. It was also a way of easing the travelling pangs of people who were coming from places so far away from Malamulo.[28] As far as people at Matandani mission and those in the surrounding areas can recollect, the camp meeting of 1933 was memorable. All church members in the out-stations under Matandani mission such as Nyambi, Malimba, Lipase, Chimango and Chugai in Mozambique as had been the case in the past, came to the meeting. Perhaps it was the presence of W.H. Brandon, then the president of the EAD, who had come as the guest speaker, that put an added importance to the meeting.[29] H.M.M. Sparrow, the Malawi Union President at the time, was also present. Among the prominent African workers, whose story is described in some detail further on in this chapter, was Pastor Yokoniah Sosola who served as the camp meeting's English to Chichewa translator. Lydia Davy, the wife of the Matandani mission director was in charge of children's ministries. At the end of the camp meeting, Pastor Yokoniah Sosola baptized many people in the Nkulumadzi River.[30]

In 1934, Davy was asked to take charge of affairs at Malamulo Mission when K. Nash, the director there went on furlough. An American, E.B. Jewell from Mwami mission in Zambia,[31] came to Matandani. The

---

[27] Note that today each Adventist church conducts its own camp meeting. Members from prayer-houses attend the camp meetings of the main church under whose supervision they are.

[28] See "History of the SEAU," pp. 24-25.

[29] W.H. Branson later became the president of the GC between 1950 and 1954.

[30] Interview, Matsimbe, 25 August 1998.

[31] Although geographically in Zambia, Mwami mission located close to the border with Central Malawi was, for administrative purposes, grouped under Adventist institutions in Malawi and given the title "attached field". From the point of missionary history, E.G. Marcus pioneered the mission. This mission started primarily as a clinic. In 1925 the Malawi Union was formed and the area of the Union included Malawi as well as Mozambique between latitudes 11 and 12 and Zambia East of meridian 32. In 1927 the Malawi Union under N.C. Wilson as president, was divided into three fields: South, Central and North. The Central Field included Mwami. In fact, the director of Mwami mission was also the in-charge of the Central Malawi Field. In 1950 and 1969 Mozambique and Zambia were removed from the Malawi union, respectively. See, Gordon Doss, "Survey of the Organizational Development and Growth of the South East Africa Union,"

Jewels stayed at the mission until 1937. When they went on furlough towards the end of that year (1937), they never returned to Malawi.[32] In what had by now been a reoccurring phenomenon, Matandani mission directorship fell vacant again after Jewell left.[33] This kind of situation provided the opportunity for African workers to display their ability in managing administrative affairs not only at Matandani but also at other Adventist missions in the country. For the first time in the history of the mission, Yokoniah Sosola was appointed as the first full-time official African director of Matandani mission.

Pastor Yokoniah Sosola

Pastor Yokoniah Sosola (1885-1969),[34] apart from Pastor Morrison Malinki and Peter Nyambo, features prominently in the early history of the mission. In many ways, he was a pioneer. His appointment as director at the mission was, to say the least, an achievement that many African workers only wished for. Until his brief appointment as head of Matandani mission, few African workers in the Malawi Union had held high posts in the church. It was only missionaries, regardless of the lack of experience of some of them (for example, Byron Ellingworth who succeeded Pastor Y. Sosola as is noted later), that

---

BA research paper for the course History of the Seventh-day Adventist Church (CH 570), Andrews University, May 1974, pp. 4-6.

[32] EWEP Robinson, "Third Angel", p. 212.

[33] Virgil Robinson concurs when he states that "Matandani was another mission which has occasionally gone for many months and even years without a director," Ibid.

[34] Peter Sosola (born 1935), son of Pastor Y. Sosola, Matandani mission, 28 December 1999. For some mention of Pastor Y. Sosola see also "EWEP History of SEAU," pp. 42-43.

posts of leadership were given. Although his tenure of one year was brief, work at the mission advanced under his supervision. When a missionary director was found at the end of 1938, Pastor Sosola was transferred to Chileka mission as director and where Adzes Mb'ebuwa was the head of the mission school. At Chileka mission, Pastor Y. Sosola succeeded Pastor James Ngaiyaye upon the appointment of the latter as the first African Field Secretary in the Malawi Union at the end of 1938.

In 1940, Pastor Y. Sosola was again transferred to Thambani mission where he became the director of that mission. Towards the end of the 1940s, Pastor Y. Sosola was transferred back to Matandani, this time as the pastor of the mission. By the time he left Matandani mission in 1953, Pastor Y. Sosola had pioneered the establishment of many churches in the area, which were under the supervision of Matandani. In all, Pastor Y. Sosola worked for the Adventist church for 48 years and retired in 1958. He died in retirement on 8 November 1969.[35]

It should be observed however, that the appointment of African directors or acting directors was by default. It was only when there was a shortage of missionaries that Africans were elevated to these positions of responsibility, only to be sidelined when a missionary was found. The African directors at the mission in the two instances so far mentioned did commendable work although it should be pointed out that the time they spent in those positions of responsibilities was brief.

Byron L. Ellingworth, the son of G.A. Ellingworth arrived at Matandani mission as the new director in 1938. He had been attending Helderberg College in South Africa prior to his coming. For Byron, it had been 10 years since he was last at Matandani with his father where he had received part of his primary school education. When he returned, now as director, most of his school and classmates were still at the mission either as teachers or general workers.[36] A year later, Byron married Ferne Wilson and worked at Matandani for a few months before being transferred to Thekerani mission as its director.[37]

---

[35] Interview, Peter Sosola, 28 December 1999.
[36] Interview, Matsimbe, 24 August 1998.
[37] EWEP "History of SEAU," p. 43.

Now, for 31 years the foundations of Matandani mission had been laid. The departure of B.L. Ellingworth also signalled the end of the foundation era. For the next four years, the mission was without a missionary director and again national workers in their various capacities as pastors, evangelists, teachers, general workers and students kept the mission on its feet. Apart from the problems associated with the Chilembwe Rising, the placid years between 1915 and 1939 were punctuated by the activities of a local teacher at the mission. This was Wilfred Gudu, whose apostasy was to prove highly embarrassing for the church.

The Wilfred Gudu Affair, 1922-1925[38]

In 1935, Wilfred Gudu (1888-1963),[39] an expelled member of the Adventist church, formed an offshoot church called *Ana a Mulungu* (Children of God) in Thyolo district. Gudu's action to form an offshoot movement after a disagreement with a mother church has not been an uncommon phenomenon among African clergy and workers frustrated in the "main" churches. J. Chaphadzika Chakanza has noted that

> religious independency is always an opening for some who could not command any other sort of leadership position and even for those who could, it is often an easier and quicker route to success, providing more opportunity for self-expression, command and appreciation than any administrative or even professional roles that are available.[40]

There are, however, theological reasons why some African clergy opt for independency. Yesaya Zerenji Mwasi, originally of the Free Church of Scotland (Livingstonia mission) and later preacher and founder of the

---

[38] Unless otherwise stated, the information on Gudu (or Good as the name appears in the Zomba archival document) is based on the account of S.J. Kaphale whose father J. Kaphale was a student when Gudu was at Matandani mission. Interview, S. Kaphale, 25 August 1998.

[39] The historical reconstruction of Gudu's activities in this study is different from the one that exists in studies available and cited in this section. This account relies mainly, but not entirely, on oral sources at the mission and archival materials at the Malawi National Archives in Zomba.

[40] Chakanza, "Sectarianism in Joseph Booth's Mission Foundations, 1925-1975," p. 9.

independent denomination called "The Blackman's Church," gives poignant reasons why as an African clergy in an established church, he opted for independency. In one of the issues he raised, he states that

> I wish to save my fellow natives or to detract their mind from the erroneous idea that God is more in foreign missionaries, lands, languages, institutions, thoughts, words and actions but is less or not in the native Christianity, languages, institutions, thoughts, words and actions: that God loves white colour and hates black colour. In short that white man on account of his good surroundings is nearer God than a black man who lacks such environments. That is, another man's God, faith, thoughts or actions have no personal appeal to me nor are my personal properties or virtues. Real and personal Christianity of the soul shall begin in members of the native churches when they believe *in an indigenous and personal God*, who is with them, with their native agents, in their country, hearts, thoughts, words and actions in the truest sense He is with some other races.[41]

Added to the Gudu apostasy and breakaway, the Adventist church in Malawi has experienced a series of breakaways by expelled members who have formed independent churches. In 1941, Saulosi Chandiwiri Ngwira formed "The African Light Church (*Mpingo wa Kuunika*)" in Mzimba. Peter Nyambo founded, two years later, the "Ethiopian Universal Church" in 1943 in Ntcheu.[42] In 1946 S. Chiwanda formed the "African Thamanda Church" in Blantyre. Joseph Mphambala of Chilomoni in Blantyre was most likely a former SDA member when he founded "The African Ancestors Church" (*Chipembedzo cha Makolo Achikuda*) in 1958.[43]

In general, the SDA church has had its share of splinter groups emanating from the main body of the church.[44] Around the time of the

---

[41] Yesaya Zerenji Mwase, *Essential and Paramount Reasons for Working Independently*, Blantyre: CLAIM-Kachere, (new edition) 1999, p. 15.

[42] Note that this is the same Peter Nyambo mentioned earlier.

[43] See J. Chaphadzika Chakanza, "An Annotated List of Independent Churches in Malawi 1900-1981", *Sources for the Study of Religion in Malawi* (Zomba), Number 10, December 1983.

[44] For a brief analysis of these splinter groups see Schwarz, *Light Bearers*, pp. 450-454.

First World War, two such groups, one in Germany called the German Reform Movement (1915) and another in America called the Reformed Seventh-day Church (1916) were formed by former Adventist members. Although later, Margaret Rowen, the leader of the American group was discredited; she had gone as far as to claim that she had received visions like those of Ellen G. White. Of particular note in the "reformed" Adventist theology of Margaret Rowen apart from the claim that the 144,000 righteous people at the end of time would only come from the United States, was that the literal advent of Christ was to fall on 6 February 1925. Other splinter Seventh-day Adventist movements in America included the Davidian Seventh-day Adventists (1920s) and the Sanctuary Awakening Fellowship (1960s).[45] Even the sect (led by David Koresh) that ended in tragedy at Waco, Texas in 1993 had some Adventist background.[46] Although there is no evidence to suggest that these developments in America and Germany (notably those up to the 1920s) had any influence on Gudu in Malawi, the missionaries at Matandani mission who were likely aware of these developments outside Africa, may have found Gudu's attitude and actions disturbing.

The story of Wilfred Gudu is both political and religious but only issues leading up to his activities at Matandani mission are the emphasis of this study.[47] A Mang'anja by ethnicity, Gudu's first contact with the

---

[45] Splits from the Seventh-day Adventist church nowhere reached larger numbers, neither in the North nor in Malawi.

[46] David Koresh, whose real name was Vernon Howell, was the leader of a fanatical religious sect that split from an Adventist splinter group known as the Branch Davidians. It were the members of the Branch Davidians who were former members of the SDA church before being dropped from SDA membership in November 1930. Koresh's sect ended in tragedy when he and his followers had a shoot out with America's Alcohol, Tobacco and Firearms (AFT) agents, in Waco, Texas on 15 March 1993. See Colin D. Standout, "Lessons from Waco," and Monterrey, "Waco: Insights on the Davidian Movement part 1," *Our Firm Foundation*, volume 8, Number 6, June 1993, pp. 4-7 and pp. 14-17, respectively.

[47] The political aspect of Gudu's independent church included objections to the payment of hut tax and a ban on its members in following government policies on soil conservation. For these "strange" religious teachings, Gudu had a showdown with the colonial authority resulting in his imprisonment and that of some of his followers. See some aspects of this account in Joseph C. Chakanza, *Voices of Preachers in Protest: The Ministry of two Malawian Prophets: Elliot Kamwana and Wilfred Gudu*, Blantyre: CLAIM-Kachere, 1998, pp. 58-82.

Adventist church was when he enrolled at Malamulo Mission School in 1906. In 1911 while still at Malamulo, he was baptized into the church. It appears that Gudu was a good student academically. The fact that the Adventists offered him a teaching appointment soon after completing his primary studies in 1911 attests to this. His character, though, is difficult to ascertain. More likely, he was a kind of person easily stung to indignant action if he felt that his status as an educated person and an African for that matter was undermined. To some of the teachers in his primary school days, he was thought of as a person who loved self-exaltation. At Malamulo Mission School, he went through the hands of teachers like the black American lady, Mabel Branch (up to 1907), Joel Rogers (as from 1907) and Malawians such as Philip Masonga, Simon Ngaiyaye and James Malinki.[48]

In 1918, he was sent to teach at Msomera School, an Adventist outschool formerly owned by Malinki and situated at Malabvi near Limbe. While at Msomera, it is alleged that he temporarily went insane and wondered in the bush nude for several weeks. For three years after that incident he continued to teach at the school. In 1921, he was transferred to Matandani Mission School at the time G.A. Ellingworth was the director there.

Missionaries at Matandani like most white people in Malawi at that time insisted that Africans dress and conduct themselves in a particularly inferior way in their presence. Of particular importance to many of these white people was the demand that Africans wearing hats raise them at the approach of a white person as a sign of respect. It should be noted that one of the frustrations of John Chilembwe against white people in general, was this patronizing attitude.[49] Gudu like Chilembwe resented this requirement. At the mission, he found missionaries strictly forbidding African workers, teachers and students to "wear shoes and hats in public as their non-African counterparts did."[50] On a number of occasions, Gudu ignored these restrictions to the obvious anger of the missionaries. It was clear from the start that Gudu's stay at Matandani would be rocky.

---

[48] See ibid., pp. 63-65.
[49] See Shepperson and Price, *Independent African*, p. 369.
[50] Chakanza, Voices of Preachers in Protest, p. 64.

At Matandani, Gudu noticed another problem that he also resented. Most African leading posts at the mission were in the hands of Ngoni members of the church.[51] As a Mang'anja, he observed that even in cases where a Mang'anja or a Lomwe should have been promoted, that did not happen and instead, a Ngoni was usually promoted. Gudu resented this Ngoni domination and spoke out against it to the obvious displeasure of the missionaries and the Ngoni staff at the mission. The Ngoni factor should be put into the perspective of the early years of the Adventist church in Malawi. In his 1972 paper, Cedric Khanje outlined three theories that attempt to explain the Ngoni domination of leading posts in the entire Malawi Union, a phenomenon evident even today.[52]

One theory is that Lomwe or Mang'anja unlike the Ngoni, "even when educated tended to be tenacious to traditional practices such as *nsembe* and initiation" practices anathema to Adventist beliefs. Therefore, many Lomwe and Mang'anja workers failed to meet church standards because

> the church has a quasi-intelligence system which gives information about each officer's behaviour. Most officials are drawn from field teachers. When Lomwe teachers continue to send sons for initiation, such matters come up when individuals are screened before a promotion is made. The church promotes people who will give a good image of the church to the public.[53]

To illustrate this, in his survey Khanje found out that of the eleven African directors at Mbalanguzi station from its inception in 1921 until the time of the survey in 1972, all were Ngoni except three.[54]

Another theory is that by the 1920s, the majority of well-educated African workers were Ngoni. The explanation is that, at Malamulo Mission

---

[51] It should be noted that the Ngoni alluded to the argument in this section are referring to the Ngoni peoples from the Ntcheu area and were employed by the church and sent to work at Matandani. It is possible that some Ntumba-Ngoni working at Matandani mission at that time were also at an advantage over Mang'anja and Lomwe workers.

[52] See Khanje, "Impact of Malamulo Mission", pp. 7-10.

[53] Ibid., p. 8.

[54] This study has also found out that the Ngoni domination theory in the Adventist church is relevant today. All the African principals at the mission between 1971 and 1989 have been Ngoni. See the appendices for details.

School where most of them trained, the Ngoni who came from far away in the Central Region, tended to work harder and were more serious in academic work than their Lomwe or Mang'anja classmates. Mang'anja and Lomwe tended to be complacent allegedly because the school was in their area. Many of these tended to desert classes, break curfews and ended up being expelled from school. As a consequence of this, more Ngoni members of the church were educated and small wonder that their percentage as employed workers of the church was greater than that of the Mang'anja or Lomwe. Yet another theory suggests that when Malinki's schools were amalgamated with the Adventist out-schools, his teachers, most of them Ngoni, automatically became SDA church employees. It is also likely that as the inspector of SDA schools from 1908 until 1921, as earlier noted, Malinki, in recommending workers for various higher officers, tended to favour Ngoni workers.

In 1922 Wilfred Gudu, tired of the Ngoni domination and the attitude of the missionaries towards African workers in general, went around in secret to interest especially Mang'anja and Lomwe workers to support him in openly protesting against the state of affairs at the mission. Unfortunately for him, he got no support from those he thought he was representing. When his activities became known, the mission administration convened to take disciplinary action against him. One problem though was the fact that there was no direct concrete evidence against him for his alleged "rebellious" acts. Perhaps what saved him was the attitude of the other African workers at the mission. In his observation of African members at Matandani mission around this time, S.G. Maxwell found out that

> the (sic) Africans were reticent to sit in judgement on their brethren, even though they had apostatized. They were still "our brother." In fact, once elected to an office, they imagined they always retain that title. People would be addressed as deacons long after they had vacated that office. It was hard to change an elder. A chief or headman who had given land for a church

always referred to it as his church, even though he was still a polygamist.[55]

If Maxwell's view can be taken at face value, then it can be suggested that Gudu escaped the "wrath" of the church because of this attitude by the local members, something that missionaries found disturbing. This observation may also lead one to conclude that this attitude was a subtle reaction by African members against the way missionaries at times treated them. In general, Gudu's actions were unwelcome at the mission. From available sources, it would appear that many people at the mission saw Gudu's action as an attempt not at addressing a genuine concern but rather as a way of bringing schism into the church. To most of these people, the view was that Gudu wanted recognition beyond that of a teacher and that his attempt to lead out in the protest was a way of drawing attention to himself.[56]

Although there was lack of direct evidence against him for allegedly engaging himself in schismatic activities, the mission administration was convinced that Gudu's actions since his arrival at the mission would harm the church. Especially Gudu's attitude and relationship with missionaries since his arrival at the mission, a year before, the administration had become convinced that Gudu was a troublemaker. However, the lack of concrete evidence against him for these allegations saved Gudu from being immediately expelled from the church and dismissed from employment. As the policy of the church stands, if there was substantiated evidence that he was indeed guilty of these allegations, he could have been expelled from the church. The Adventist church is serious about cases of its members displaying divisive attitudes. The Adventist Church Manual makes the position of the church on such matters clear. It states that

> although all members have equal rights within the church, no individual member or group of members should start a movement or form an organization or seek to encourage a following

---

[55] Maxwell, *I Loved Africa*, p. 119.
[56] See MNA, The Good file S43/1/18/1.

for the attainment of any objective or for the teaching of any doctrine or message not in harmony with the fundamental religious objectives and teachings of the Seventh-day Adventist Church. Such a course would result in the fostering of a factional and divisive spirit, in the fragmenting of the effort and witness of the church, and thus in hindering it in the discharge of its obligations to its Head and to the world.[57]

What followed next was that Gudu was told that he should no longer teach or evangelize but instead work at the mission's maintenance workshop as a casual labourer. That Gudu was demoted from teacher to casual worker immediately after his differences with the mission administration leads one to conclude that he was being victimized because of his pro-Mang'anja/Lomwe and anti-colonial/Ngoni activities at the mission.[58]

Sources at the mission further reveal that it was when Gudu was working in that demoted position that two other skills he knew, cloth making and dyeing, were put to good use. It is unclear from available sources as from where Gudu had learnt these skills. It is likely that he learnt them at Malamulo Mission School during his student days. It should be noted that Gudu's independent church eventually developed into a religious institution that cut itself off from ordinary aspects of life, a unique feature in the understanding of independent churches in Malawi. In Gudu's quasi-religious community, both religious piety and industrial activities were emphasized. So it can be seen that Gudu had a number of industrial skills that he later found of great use in his peculiar type of religious independency.[59]

After the demotion, Gudu remained at Matandani mission and in his spare-time began to teach interested students how to dye and make cloth from raw cotton, activities that appeared to have made him popular

---

[57] *The Seventh-day Adventist Church Manual* (15th edition), Maryland: Review and Herald Publishing Association, 1995, p. 164.

[58] Some sources say that after his demotion, Gudu worked as a casual labourer in the carpentry section of the maintenance department. Interview, S.J. Kaphale, 25 August 1998.

[59] See Chakanza, Voices of Preachers in Protest, pp. 58-66.

with students. For example, Gudu taught J. Kaphale, the father of one of the leading informants in this study, to make cloth from raw cotton. His popularity annoyed the missionaries who thought that by demoting him, they had put him in his "right place" and squashed his haughtiness. Other African teachers especially Ngoni, were also not amused by the fact that Gudu was still drawing attention to himself. These teachers passed sneering comments saying that the skills Gudu was teaching were inferior levels of training unlike the more academic subjects they were teaching.[60]

The last straw in the shaky relationship between Gudu and the mission administration came in 1925 when there was no missionary at the mission after the departure of W.L. Davy. The responsibility to deal with Gudu then remained with the church pastor and his church-board, many of whom were Ngoni. In this instance, Gudu intervened by speaking out in a case of adultery of some members. The man involved in the case was expelled. Gudu felt that the man was treated unfairly by the mission authorities and spoke out. When the Matandani mission church-board convened, it unanimously agreed that Gudu was a threat to church discipline at the mission. It was then decided to expel him from membership of the church and, in line with SDA church policy, Gudu automatically lost his church employment as well.[61]

Gudu filed a complaint against the action, but the mission ignored him. After this, he demanded $175.10 compensation for unfair dismissal and as gratuity for the years of service he had given to the church. The mission again ignored him. Even his appeal to the president of the Union, G.A. Ellingworth yielded nothing. Gudu retreated to his home area in Headman Khwetumule's village and settled at Kaponda village not far

---

[60] S.J. Kaphale, 25 August 1998.

[61] In the SDA church, expelled members lose their employment if the individual is a church worker as well. In all such cases, the church-board must first establish whether the person in question has apostatized. The employing organization then makes a decision after the spiritual aspect has been dealt with. In a recent (1997) case at Matandani mission, a boarding-mistress in charge of female students who is a widow began a relationship that became non-platonic with another male worker at the mission, also a widower. When it was established that the two were secretly cohabiting, the mission's church-board met and decided to disfellowship both of them. The school then dismissed them from employment.

away from Malamulo mission. Between 1925 and 1935, he continued to seek a response to his claim for compensation. Even his appeal to the director of Malamulo mission, G.R. Nash, between these years was unsuccessful. In 1935, he appealed to the DC about the matter. Not taking him seriously, the DC, W.D. Phillips, suggested that if he was not happy with the Adventist church, he could start his own. In the same year, Gudu founded the *Ana a Mulungu* Church.[62]

Gudu's break with the Adventist church owes much to his activities at Matandani mission. His demotion and later dismissal from employment made worse by the refusal of the church leadership to re-address his case left him bitter. Gudu could have re-entered a Bible class and then be re-baptized if he had wanted to rejoin the church, but Gudu chose to form a breakaway church. In his peculiar type of independent church, it appears that he adopted the more extreme beliefs of the Adventist church and then added some of his own beliefs based on his interpretation of the Bible.

It can be observed that the beliefs and teachings of most independent churches, whose founders were former Adventists, tend to break the permitted bounds of religious expression. It is as if these new churches try to outdo even the strictest beliefs of the mother church. For example, David Koresh and his Branch Davidians believed that Armageddon would begin after the conversion of the Jews by means of violent force.[63] Another example is Peter Nyambo. When he returned to Malawi in 1943 from South Africa as an old man, he founded an independent church based on the teachings of Sri Ramakrishna, a concept combining what is best in all religions.[64] Finally, although Gudu's church managed to establish small communities in Thyolo, Mulanje, Ntcheu and Mwanza

---

[62] See Chakanza, *Voices of Preachers in Protest*, p. 65 and also Chakanza, "An Annotated List."

[63] Monterrey, "Waco" pp. 14-15. There are differing views among Adventists as to what Armageddon really means. The mainstream view is that this will be a spiritual battle between good and evil. Other Adventists however view it as a literal military engagement to come between God's people and those of Satan. See Schwarz, *Light Bearers*, pp. 402-403.

[64] See Shepperson and Price, *Independent African*, p. 413.

districts, its "fame" seems to have been synonymous with its clashes with the government over the land conservation policies.[65]

---

[65] For other aspects of Gudu and his church see Robert B. Boeder, "Wilfrid Good and Ana a Mulungu Church," History seminar paper, Chancellor College, Zomba, 1982/83; I.H.D. Musowa, "The Ana Mulungu Church of Wilfred Gudu: Its Raison d' Etre," Theology seminar paper, Chancellor College, Zomba, 1981 and R.I. Rotberg, *The Rise of Nationalism in Central Africa: The Making of Malawi and Zambia: 1873-1964*, Cambridge, Ma: Harvard University Press, 1967 (especially pp. 151-155)

Chapter 3

INSTITUTIONAL DEVELOPMENT 1943 - 1971

The Work of O.I. Fields, 1943-1967

The period between 1943 and 1971 was characterized by infrastructural development at the mission. If the efforts of one person could be singled out, it would be those of the missionary Orson I. Fields who is credited with most of the infrastructural development at the mission during this period. An American family, Orlson Fields, his wife Emma and their three children (Bargeline, Webster and Davie) arrived in Malawi in 1943.[1]

Initially, the Fields came to Malawi not as missionaries for Matandani mission. They came into the country to wait for his visa to enter Mozambique as the new director of Munguluni ('Light') mission. Prior to his appointment to head Munguluni, Fields had been the director of Bongo Training School in Angola where he had perfected his Portuguese. However, when Fields and his family arrived in Blantyre, the Malawi Union informed them that there was no accommodation for a missionary family at the Union. Instead, the Union sent them to Matandani mission where a missionary house was available after the departure of B.L. Ellingworth.[2]

After waiting for some time, the Portuguese government in Mozambique refused to give the Adventist missionary a visa to enter

---

[1] Mrs. H. Mletseni, who was a young girl at the time Fields arrived at the mission, remembers the Fields' children very well because some of them were her playmates. Interview, Mrs. Mletseni, Matandani mission, 26 August 1998.

[2] Interview, F.L. Matsimbe, Matandani mission, 25 August 1998

their country. It is important to note that Fields' application to enter Mozambique was made at the height of the Second World War (1939-1945) when there were travel restrictions in many parts of the world. For historical reasons, the relationship between Portuguese and British colonial governments in Central Africa was a strained one. Towards the end of the 1800s, the two colonial powers had clashed over the ownership of the Shire Highlands.[3] Religiously, too, Portugal, a nation deeply rooted in Roman Catholicism, was averse to have non-Catholic missions in their territory. It is likely that these factors may have persuaded the Portuguese government officials in Mozambique to reject Fields' visa application. The EAD appointed Fields as the new director of Matandani as the mission had not had a missionary for four years. With an excellent *savoir-faire*, Fields was to change the face of Matandani mission.

Both Fields and his wife Emma were sturdy physically and hard workers. It was therefore natural for Fields to expect everyone around to work as hard as him. This had a double effect on the mission: the infrastructure at the mission was improved but many workers and students complained for being made to work excessively hard. Unlike all mission directors before him, Fields had one aim in mind and that was to expand and improve the mission infrastructure in the shortest time and cheapest way possible. Taking advantage of the increased student enrollment, Fields used labour from the "student mission work programme"[4] (which was part of the curriculum), and labour provided by students who could not afford school fees. These worked at various building projects at the mission. Manual work for both students and workers was intensified. According to S.J. Kaphale (a student at the mission in the 1940s) it was not unusual for students to run away from school because of the hard work that they were expected to do everyday.[5] At Malamulo mission the situation was similar because "the

---

[3] See D.E. Needham, *Iron Age to Independence: A History of Central Africa*, London: Longman, 1974, pp. 110-112.

[4] Here and frequently below "mission work" is used in its specific Seventh-day Adventist meaning: Manual work on the mission as part or in place of school fees.

[5] Interview, S.J. Kaphale, 25 August 1998.

programme [mission work] was so strenuous that many boys came, remained a week or two, and disappeared in the night!"[6]
For students, a typical day at Matandani began with mission work from early morning until lunchtime. In the afternoon students attended classes. Teachers, including the African head-teachers at the school, were also always on their toes under the direct supervision of Emma Fields. Emma Fields was a "jack of all trades" kind of person. She was both a teacher and supervisor at the primary school. She was also a nurse. When there was need, she was seen attending to patients at the little mission "hospital". She also had a working knowledge of hydrotherapy, a popular medical treatment among Adventists in America.[7] Using this method of treatment she occasionally treated lightening victims and those with boils or wounds at her house. An account given by Mrs. H. Mletseni gives an idea of the method Emma Fields used to treat such wounds. A patient with sores or cuts was told to immerse the affected part of the body in hot water. It was very painful as the water burnt on the wound but after a few days the wound was healed.[8]

The colonial government in Malawi introduced grants-in-aid that were made available to mission controlled schools. However, the government money had conditions that missions were to abide by if they were to continue receiving such aid. One such condition was that over-average or mature age students were not to be given places in schools because the government felt that it was a waste of money to subsidize students who were already too old. The government sent a circular to the effect that mission-run schools that continued to offer places to such students would risk losing the grant. In order to continue receiving the grant, Fields implemented the unpopular government policy on over-age students. Due to the large numbers of such students at Matandani

---

[6] EWEP "History of SEAU," p. 6.

[7] Developed by Dr. James C. Jackson, hydrotherapy, taught at Battle Creek Sanitarium, was an alternative method of treatment. The method of treatment relied on a system of hot baths and cooling packs, a moderate liquid diet and plentiful drinking water and thorough ventilation of the sickroom, all combined with rest and careful nursing. See Schwarz, *Light Bearers*, p. 107.

[8] Interview, Mrs. H. Mletseni, Matandani mission, 25 August 1998.

Mission School and in the surrounding schools under its supervision, the mission begun to run separate classes for over-age students. However, as government regulations tightened, over-age students were told to leave school altogether and start a family.[9]

By the start of the 1950s, the primary school offered a full primary school education. Qualified African teachers, most of them from the prestigious Malamulo Training School, filled the primary school corridors. Some of the teachers included B. Chinsinga, F.L. Matsimbe, F.M. Chapendeka, N. Chasweka, E. Zikakhana, R. Tsoka, J. Khwangwala, and T. Khonje.[10] The African head-teacher of the primary school around this time was Richard Lumala. In 1958, M.F. Nseula succeeded Lumala and would work in that capacity until 1962.[11]

Immediately he was appointed director, Fields embarked on ambitious plans to build up the mission. His father-in-law, Mr Gill, who came from America after the death of his wife, gave volunteer service at the mission. In fact, most of the projects that Fields undertook were done with the help of Mr. Gill.[12] For a long time, safe drinking water was difficult to get at the mission. Fields' first interest then, was to find a source where he could tap clean drinking water. For this venture, he went to the hills at Kaliyoni[13] and dug a well there, but unfortunately the water level was too low.

---

[9] One of the leading informants in this study, S.J. Kaphale who was a pupil at the mission at the time, told the researcher that he was one of the students who suffered because of this policy. Interview, S.J. Kaphale, 24 August 1998.

[10] Note that most of the teachers listed here were involved in a protest action against the administration of Fields in 1953. This protest is fully covered later in this chapter.

[11] After leaving Matandani Mission School, Nseula was appointed by the church to work at the Voice of Prophecy, an Adventist centre for the promotion of Adventist faith through literature. Nseula retired from church service in 1978 and is currently at his home in Neno. Interview, M.F. Nseula, retired head-teacher of Matandani Mission School, Nseula village, Neno, 28 December 1999.

[12] The local people at the mission nicknamed Mr. Gill *gogo*, the vernacular word for grandparent, because of his age

[13] This is a *Chichewa* word that had been literary translated from English. The story behind the word is that the first white people to the area (on the hills to the north of the mission) who came by *machila* kept on telling their African porters to avoid short rest stops and to keep on walking.

After this set-back he decided to pump water from the Nkulumadzi River below but the problem was to find a way of pushing it up to the mission. What Fields did to achieve this has remained one of the technological wonders ever to be undertaken at the mission. Some time at the beginning of 1953, Fields taking with him Mr. Gill, F. Matsimbe and N. Nsampha went up the Kirk Range Mountain. They went there to survey the possibility of tapping water from the source of the Nkulumadzi cataracts. The idea was to find a way of channeling the water down the mountain where the gravitational force created would pump water up to the mission. After surveying the area, Fields concluded that it was possible to tap water from the cataracts from up the source of Nkulumadzi River in the Kirk Range Mountain, through a man made canal that would wind round the hill to where the water could be forced down a steep outlet at the river below.

After a careful study, he concluded that such a project could not only supply water for domestic use at the mission but the force created at the artificial outlet would produce hydroelectric power.[14] F.L. Matsimbe says that the idea looked laughable and no one, except Fields himself, knew how this idea could be turned into reality.[15] Further research however reveals that the idea of using the cataracts to generate electricity was not new in the area. Sources indicate that Fields copied this idea from the Roman Catholic missionaries at St. Armand, who had built a similar infrastructure much earlier. In fact, Fields made several trips to the Catholic mission to learn how he could build such infrastructure at Matandani and Catholic missionaries were sometimes seen at the mission providing Fields with technical assistance.[16]

Without much outside financial assistance, Fields mobilized all the resources he had at the mission and embarked on a massive canal construction project. This project required extensive manual labour and

---

To emphasize that, they repeatedly uttered the English words "carry on". The African porters misheard them as saying "*kaliyoni*".

[14] See map at the beginning of the thesis.

[15] Interview, F.L. Matsimbe, 25 August 1998.

[16] Interview, S.F. Machilika, Registrar, Matandani Mission Secondary School, 29 December 1999.

when it began, every available labour was utilized. For students, whose labour was crucial if the project was to succeed, mission work took on an altogether new meaning. Even teachers at the mission were not spared from taking part in the project. Although they were not required to do the actual manual work, they were expected to supervise the students they taught and were further required to be with the students throughout the entire time students worked on the project. Canal digging began early in the day and would consume the whole morning. Classes were held in the afternoon. Each student was given a minimum of 12 meters of canal to dig every day. Teachers were to make sure that students they supervised finished their portions before classes could begin in the afternoon.[17] It was during this time that an African worker at the mission shot to prominence. He was Pastor J. Khwangwala.

J. Khwangwala was born in Mozambique in 1911. Together with his parents, he came into Malawi during the general migration of Mozambiquans into Malawi at the start of the twentieth century.[18] Khwangwala did his pre-primary school education at Ilemba School located at Kwamperama village in Mwanza district. For part of his early primary school, he attended Thambani Mission School. Later he walked to Malamulo where he joined the primary school there and later completed part of his primary school education. It was at Malamulo mission where he was converted and baptized into the Adventist church.

He left Malamulo Mission School in 1938 and married soon afterwards. From Malamulo mission he went to Thambani Mission School, his alma mater, where he began his teaching career. In 1945, he was transferred to Matandani Mission School where Fields had been for two years. Because of his dedication and hard work, Fields

---

[17] Interview, Matsimbe, 25 August 1998.

[18] For aspects of these migrations, see Andrew Ross, *Blantyre Mission and the Making of Modern Malawi*, Blantyre: CLAIM-Kachere, 1996, p. 15; N. Northup, "The Migrations of the Yao and Kololo into Southern Malawi: Aspects of Migrations in Nineteenth Century Africa, *International Journal of African Studies*, vol. 19, no. 1 (1986), pp. 55-75.

recommended to the church that he be ordained.[19] After his ordination, he took upon an added career as a pastor.[20]

Immediately he arrived at Matandani, Pastor Khwangwala became Fields' favourite African worker mainly because of his dedication to work. A common story at the mission is that the two men were so close as friends that of all the African workers at the mission, it was only Khwangwala, who could go into Fields' house, enter through any door at any time and demand food from the cook! This was unheard of in colonial Malawi where parameters of contact between the races (and white being superior) were strictly adhered to, even in the SDA church. When Fields retired in 1967, he sold one of his vehicles at a give away price to Khwangwala. Manuel Nzume who was at the time Fields' domestic servant says that there was actually a strong rumour that when he would retire, Fields would take Khwangwala and his family to the United States.[21] This, though, did not happen. Today (2000), Pastor Khwangwala, who retired in the late 1970s, is living in Mwanza district.

By the time the canal digging project started, Fields had already elevated Khwangwala to the position of African supervisor at the mission. Fields also made him the first African preceptor (i.e. one in charge of the student affairs). So influential was Khwangwala at the mission that it is alleged that no African could approach Fields without first talking to him. Since Fields depended on him very much, he was taught all the important skills (e.g. driving the mission tractor) to enable him to effectively supervise work at the mission. To speed up the canal-digging

---

[19] Mrs. Ethel Botomani (nee Khwangwala), Matandani mission, 23 August 1998.

[20] Note that in the early years of the SDA church in Malawi, no one could go on his own wish to train as a pastor. The church got its pastors through a carefully monitored system. Only those who were already working for the church, say as teachers or general workers, and had proven their utmost dedication to the church and had shown a thorough knowledge of the church's doctrines, who were recommended for pastoral training or who were ordained as pastors. In this way, some church workers were ordained without necessarily going through pastoral training. Most African church workers, who eventually became pastors, had been teachers first. In fact for many years, the teaching profession was the main avenue for African church workers to enter the pastorate. It was the greatest wish of every worker to be chosen to go for pastoral training or to be ordained.

[21] Interview, Manuel Nzume, Matandani mission, 25 August 1998.

project, Fields gave incentives of used clothes to students who completed their portions on time. This was also done to encourage them to take on more portions before classes began in the afternoon. The canal, measuring about six kilometers in length, was finally completed in 1956.[22] Now the mission had a steady supply of drinking water and hydroelectric power. The introduction of the latter helped in powering the industrial training school machines.

To raise money for the mission in the effort to make the school self-sufficient, O.I. Fields accepted to do external projects, taking advantage of the huge human resource he had. A new road from Mwanza turn-off to Neno was started in the 1950s by the government. Sources at the mission indicate that Fields won a government contract to clear that road. Student labour was used in the road project. Like with the canal project, students were expected to complete a certain portion every morning as a prerequisite to attend classes in the afternoon. Although some oral sources indicate that Fields used the money from this contract for his personal use, it is most likely that he invested the money into other mission projects.[23]

Fields realized that if the mission was to be self-sufficient in food especially for boarding students, work at the mission gardens was to be intensified and carefully monitored. He made Pastor Khwangwala farm supervisor in addition to other responsibilities he had. On his part, Pastor Khwangwala became infamous for his strictness and occasional beatings of students who were thought to be lazy at the farm. Work at the mission farm was strenuous and would go on until lunchtime. Classes were held in the afternoon but only after a student had completed a morning's portion of work at the farm. Teachers, like on the canal project and other projects, were expected to supervise the students they taught. Work at the farm was tough and just the thought of the farm could strike fear and

---

[22] Interview, Matsimbe, 25 August 1998.

[23] S.F. Machilika alleges that Fields used some of the money for his own use. According to him, Fields bought a custom-made Mercedes Benz when he went back to America on retirement. Interview, Matandani mission, 23 August 1998. Although this study cannot confirm this allegation, various people interviewed for this study maintain the view that Fields kept some of the money he was given for mission projects by his American sponsors for his own personal use.

resentment in a student. Not surprisingly, the mission farm was aptly called mlangamfiti[24] like the Malamulo farm. On Malamulo farm, Cedrick Khanje observed that "at mlangamfiti, a pupil had to finish his (sic) allotted task or else starve that day, since the policy was no satisfactory work, no lunch, no classes."[25]

The intensity and nature of manual work required of students on the canal, road clearing and at the farm made students twist the name Matandani to read mnyamatandani.[26] Apart from this negativity, Fields was putting this labour to good use. The aging infrastructure at the mission received much attention. New houses for teachers and married students, who came to attend the industrial school when it was started in 1953, were constructed. All remaining mission wattle and daub structures were replaced with burnt bricks. A project to roof all mission buildings with tiles was also undertaken. By the early 1960s, most of the roofs of the mission buildings were covered in red tiles. Many of the buildings at the mission today are still roofed with these tiles. Between 1960 and 1966 a dispensary, the primary school as it stands today and an elaborate church were constructed. The church that can easily seat 600 people was styled after the church of Solusi University in Bulawayo, Zimbabwe.

To raise money for mission projects and cover some daily expenses, Fields built three maize-mills around the mission. The one built at the mission was run by electricity from the hydroelectric plant. The other two, one at Mitundu and the other at Njawe, used diesel. Payment for grinding maize at these mills was accepted both in cash and in giving part of the maize as payment. According to Manuel Nzume, in a good month the mission could collect between eight and ten bags of maize from grinders who paid for milling services with maize.[27] It was the heavy mission work for students and the demand that teachers be student-work supervisors that was most resented by African teachers. Having ignored to address

---

[24] Literally meaning in English "punishing witches/wizards."
[25] Khanje, "Impact of Malamulo Mission," p. 7.
[26] Meaning "who is the person to withstand the toil." Interview, S.J. Kaphale, 25 August 1998.
[27] Interview, Nzume, 25 August 1998.

their complaints, African teachers went into open protest against Fields and his administration.

African Teachers' Protest of 1953[28]

In March 1953, African teachers at Matandani mission sent a petition of protest to O.I. Fields demanding an end to the requirement that teachers supervise mission work of the students they taught. They threatened that if their demand was not met by 1 April 1953 they would stop working as teacher-supervisors. Underlining this complaint was the protest that mission work was excessively demanded on students. Although mission work had been done even before Fields came, there was a general complaint that Fields had little regard for African workers and students whom he pushed to work like drought animals. What appears to have contributed to the frustration of many African teachers was the unsubstantiated rumour about Fields receiving funds from America for projects but keeping it for his personal use.

Although the protest at Matandani mission was unique, dissatisfaction among African SDA workers has a long history in Malawi. The first African protest took place at Malamulo mission in 1910. There, African teachers had complained of being given heavy teaching loads but with little remuneration of only 10 shillings a month. Added to this was the obligation that all teachers work side by side with their students at the mission farm. Because of these conditions of work, many teachers at Malamulo resigned and left the mission.[29] However, unlike the Malamulo teachers, their counterparts at Matandani did not resign but stood up and openly expressed their dissatisfaction.[30]

---

[28] The information in this section, unless otherwise stated, is largely from the oral information of F. L. Matsimbe, and S.J. Kaphale, Matandani mission, 25 and 26 August 1998.

[29] See Bilima, "The SDA in Malawi," p. 77.

[30] Note that in 1991 some teachers at Malamulo Secondary School namely: Garnet Gwembere, Patrick Mbewe, Thengo Kumpumula, Steven Msowoya and Charles Tsakala protested against the manner in which the new principal, M. Kadyakapita, addressed their concerns. Instead of being a fair arbitrator in the feud, the Malawi Union resolved to support the view of the principal. The concerned teachers reacted by resigning from their teaching posts. It should be noted that most members of Malamulo church-board at the time tried to mediate but the Union warned them not to be involved. Identity of source withheld on request.

Why African teachers at Matandani were tenacious in openly protesting against what concerned them can perhaps be understood in the context of the political developments within and outside Malawi around that time. Being reasonably educated it is likely that news of Central African nationalists whose activities were known around that time were carefully digested. In 1949, delegations of white settlers from Malawi, Zambia and Zimbabwe met at Victoria Falls and agreed on the formation of a Federation of these three territories in spite of strong protests from Africans. In October 1953, the Federation formally came into existence and would last until 1963. African dislike of the Federation was seen through protests that took place in the three territories. In Malawi, chiefs joined in the protest because they feared that the Federation would rob them of their powers as rulers. Chief Gomani of Ntcheu in Malawi for example, came out in the open and expressed his protest to the Federation. For this, he was briefly detained. In August 1953, two months before the Federation was formally adopted, violent clashes were reported in Thyolo district where eleven people were killed and seventy-two injured.[31]

The impact of these political developments in Malawi was far reaching. Africans in the country were convinced that colonial rule was at best diabolical and the only thing that could be done to rout this evil was to drive the colonialists out. At some Christian missions, Africans formed debating clubs where contemporary issues such as social development and politics were popular.[32] By speaking out openly against British rule, Africans in general, had broken their long silence. Now time had come for the African to determine and shape his own destiny. Ironically, when the political situation was carefully analyzed, missionaries were found to

---

[31] See Needham, *Iron Age to Independence*, pp. 157-165. - For an insider account of these developments see Robert Rotberg (ed.), *Hero of the Nation. Chipembere of Malawi. An Autobiography*, Blantyre: CLAIM-Kachere, 2001.

[32] This was the case at Blantyre mission. There, missionaries allowed African workers, mostly teachers, to form civil debating clubs and deliberate on such topics. It is small wonder that missionaries were accused of fermenting African grievances that culminated in the John Chilembwe Rising of 1915. See Silas Ncozana *Sangaya: A Leader in the Synod of Blantyre Church of Central Africa Presbyterian*, Blantyre: CLAIM-Kachere (second edition, revised), 1999, p. 28.

be a part of the colonial problem. For example, the 1916 Commission of Inquiry into the disturbances in Malawi following the Chilembwe Rising outlined this connection well. The commission found out that as part of a total European culture, they (government, settlers, businesspersons and missionaries) were all, in some sense, responsible for the situation that developed in Malawi at that time.[33]

Malawi has a long history of labour migration, a phenomenon that continues to this day.[34] In some ways it was the experience that Malawians had in the countries they went to work that reinforced an antipathetic attitude against colonialism in general and white rule in particular. Men from Neno like in most parts of the country followed the tradition of going to work in the mines and farms mainly in Zimbabwe and South Africa. While there, these men experienced the worst indignities of white rule. In Zimbabwe and South Africa, the men had a first hand experience of institutionalized discrimination where Africans were required to carry passes to travel or to be in a certain place in the very country of their birth. A revolutionary attitude against white rule was surely developed by these experiences. Matandani mission did not escape the impact of these experiences. Some of the mission's former students who had gone to the mines returned and joined the mission as workers. For example F. Matsimbe, the main informant in this study who had gone to Zimbabwe and returned in 1951, joined Matandani Mission School as a teacher.[35] It is quite likely that the event that took place at the mission in 1953 was also influenced by the migrant experience.

---

[33] Quoted in Shepperson and Price, *Independent African*, p. 387.

[34] For a fuller discussion of the history of labour migration in Malawi see Robert B. Boeder, "Malawians Abroad: The History of Labour Migration from Malawi to its Neighbours 1890-1974," PhD, Michigan State University, 1974.

[35] F.L. Matsimbe, although at the ripe age of 87 at the time of the interview, proved to be a reliable source. His memory of the events he described did not leave doubt in the researcher that it was unreliable. In fact, this researcher found him on two occasions digging in his garden. Mr Matsimbe also proved the reliability of his memory by writing on a piece of paper some elements of the issue covered in this section. Matsimbe, one of the early African workers came to the mission as a young boy in 1922. He received his primary school training there. For a brief period, he went to Bulawayo, Zimbabwe where he worked on white farms as a labourer. By the late 1940s, he was back at the mission where he was employed as a teacher. F. L. Matsimbe,

The protest was the brainchild of a teacher at the mission named Bizek Chinsinga, a Lomwe by ethnicity like Gudu.[36] Chinsinga managed to convince five other teachers to join him in this protest. These were: F. Matsimbe, F.M. Chapendeka, N. Chasweka, R. Tsoka and E. Zikankhana (later called Kalulu). In the middle of March 1953, Chinsinga called these teachers to a meeting where they agreed to write a letter of complaint to Fields. The thrust of the letter was that the requirement of supervising student mission work by teachers should be scrapped or teachers would go on strike on 1 April. Such bold steps by Africans in a protest action against white rule were poignantly expressed by one of Malawi's great nationalist, Masauko Chipembere, five years later. On 4 July 1958, he stated that

> anything like moderation will never get us anywhere: whether we demand things in strong terms or whether we demand things in mild language we get nothing ... The only language which British imperialism can understand is the language of extreme conflict.[37]

Although not as extreme as Chipembere's ideas, the protesting six teachers choose Edison Zikankhana to write the letter because his written English was better than that of most of the other teachers. All protesting teachers signed the letter but used unusual names to make it difficult for anyone to identify them in case the protest went sour. The assumed names were also written in a circle for the purpose of making it difficult for the mission to easily identify the leader of the protest. The

---

who resides near Matandani mission, is an eyewitness of the long missionary history of Matandani mission especially the era of Fields. Interview, Matsimbe, 26 August 1998.

[36] Those interviewed about him say that Bizek Chinsinga was a politically minded person. After the Matandani issue he was transferred to teach at Thekerani mission school where he stayed briefly before joining government service as an agriculture officer. He later joined politics and served between 1987 and 1992 as the Member of Parliament for Thyolo South. Much of the biographical detail of B. Chinsinga is based on the oral account of his son Henry Chinsinga (born 1957) who is now resident in Gaborone, Botswana and F.L. Matsimbe quoted in the previous sections. The interviews with Henry Chinsinga took place between 15 and 16 August 1999.

[37] Needham, Iron Age to Independence, p. 172.

letter was sent to Fields by hand and a copy was posted to the Malawi Union.

Fields was not at his house when the letter came through because he had gone to Mwanza turn-off where he was supervising students in the project to clear the new Mwanza-Neno road. The letter found Emma Fields who, upon reading the letter, became immediately convinced that Edison Zikankhana wrote it. What made her suspicious of Zikankhana's involvement were the nature of the handwriting and the style of writing, especially the good English in the letter. Immediately, Emma Fields went to Zikankhana's house where she confronted him. She expressed her utmost disappointment that him of all the teachers, could join, according to her, such a 'bunch of savages' at a time when the mission had plans to send him to Domasi for further training. This psychology seems to have worked on Zikankhana because he panicked and told Emma Fields of his involvement in the affair and further revealed who was behind the whole situation. Emma Fields then rushed off to Mwanza turn-off to inform her husband of what was happening at the mission.

Upon receiving the letter and hearing news of the preliminary investigation which Emma Fields had made, her husband immediately went to the Union office in Blantyre where he had a meeting with the acting Union President and Union Treasurer, P. Stevenson. In his opinion, Fields told Stevenson, all the protesting teachers should be dismissed. Stevenson disagreed and advised that nothing should be done about the issue until the arrival of the new Union President, A.W. Austin who was due to arrive shortly. In the meantime at the mission, word of the protest had gone around among the African staff. Apart from the remaining protesting five teachers, other African teachers at the mission who incidentally were closer to the missionaries, like J. Khwangwala and T. Khonje, condemned it. When Zikankhana's betrayal became known, the other teachers in the protest promised to kill anyone in the group who would follow Zikankhana's action.[38]

In the morning of the following day, Fields summoned all the protesting teachers to his house that also served as his office. To this

---

[38] Matsimbe, 25 August 1998.

important meeting, he also invited Mr Mvundura,[39] the inspector of Matandani out-schools and Pastor Yokoniah Sosola, who was then pastor of Matandani church. Also present at this meeting were Emma Fields, Mr. Gill, E. Zikankhana and J. Khwangwala. The leader of the protest, B. Chinsinga arrived late for the meeting because early that morning he had escorted his expectant wife who was going to Blantyre. Fields interpreted Chinsinga's late-coming as deliberate. At the meeting, Fields had few words for the protesters. As far as he was concerned, they were all dismissed as teachers at the mission. The teachers were told to return school materials like books and were given a few days to vacate mission residences.

In disbelief, the teachers went to Blantyre to see Stevenson who was equally dismayed to learn that Fields had ignored his advice. Stevenson told them that according to church policy, Fields had no authority to dismiss anyone. The teachers were told to return to the mission and await a personal visit by the new Union President, who would make the Matandani debacle his priority. The policy of the SDA church regarding appointment and dismissal of workers is understood to be that a person is a member of the church first before he/she is employed in the church as a teacher, nurse etc. As noted earlier in the case of Wilfred Gudu in chapter 2, it is only when a worker has apostatized and is expelled from the church that the employing church organization can dismiss the individual from church employment.[40] The situation however is different if a church worker has not apostatized but has working differences with the supervisors of his employing church organization. In such situations, it has been observed that the concerned worker even if fired or resigns does not lose church membership.[41]

---

[39] F.L. Matsimbe noted to the author that Mr Mvundura, while in the presence of Fields, appeared to condemn the protest but in private told them to be pertinacious.

[40] Although this is the standard policy in church, it does not apply to workers who are not members of the church. Due to lack of trained staff in some church organizations like the hospitals, non-members are employed.

[41] Note the case of the Malamulo Secondary School teachers in 1991 in footnote 29 in this chapter.

Stevenson cabled Austin and urged him to hurry his arrival as the situation at Matandani was getting out of hand. Austin, who was replacing S.G. Maxwell, replied that he was arriving on 1 April. Since Matandani mission is close to the Malawi-Zimbabwe via Tete road, he announced that he would visit the mission first before proceeding to Blantyre. Stevenson informed Fields and all parties involved that they should be at Matandani on 1 April for a crisis meeting. Indeed, Austin was at Matandani by the morning of 1 April, incidentally on the day the teachers had said they would embark on the strike. The official ceremony began at around nine o'clock in the morning with a general welcome ceremony for all mission residents, teachers and students who gathered at the mission grounds. The vernacular hymn number 229 was deliberately selected. The first stanza of the song reads: "*Who is on the Lord's side? Choose on whose side you shall be*" (author's translation).[42] Even the biblical text Fields read was deliberately chosen. He read the entire third chapter of James. Although the chapter condemns disobedience, it also contains reconciliatory insinuations.[43]

After the welcoming ceremony, all concerned in the impending strike gathered in Fields' house for formal discussions to begin. Probably because of what Fields told him in camera soon after his arrival, Austin opened the meeting by lashing out at what he called "the unchristian" actions of the protesting teachers. He went on to say that the teachers should have spoken to Fields, their immediate supervisor first, before writing him and the Union letters. The protesters were reminded that as Adventist teachers, they were also evangelists. Austin's tirade lasted six hours. It was only towards the end of his speech that he asked the protesting teachers what their grievances were. The teachers mentioned several issues that grieved them. They complained about the excessive burden and the almost unbearable manual work for students. They claimed that such heavy work contributed to poor performance in class, tardiness and in some cases was the cause for student misdemeanor.

---

[42] In Chichewa, the first stanza of the song reads: "*Wa Yesuyu ndani? Ngoona; Mbali ndi ziwiri; Usankhe.*" See *Khristu mu Nyimbo*, published by Malamulo Publishing House, Makwasa, Thyolo, (no date), p. 111.

[43] See the Revised Standard Version of the Bible.

The teachers went on to complain that they had the feeling that they were themselves on some sort of punishment. The requirement that they should supervise the mission work of students they taught was, to say the least, loathed. The protesting teachers maintained that they were teachers and not casual workers. Due to the intensity of mission work, teachers complained that they did not have time to write schemes and records of work or mark students' exercises. They also complained that they did not have time to themselves and to their families. From Sunday to Sunday teachers were on duty. Even on Saturday, the Sabbath, they were expected to evangelize among their students or in the neighboring areas. The teachers revealed that some students who could not bear the heavy mission work had left school altogether. Lack of respect and sensitivity by Fields were also mentioned as areas of complaint. For example, on issues involving them, teachers complained that they were not at all consulted. Worse was the attitude of Fields towards African teachers. They mentioned that Fields had the habit of reprimanding teachers in front of their students. The teachers' feeling was that African teachers were not being accorded the full respect and honour that teachers in other places were given.

Fields, to say the least, was dumbfounded by such tenacity from these teachers. On several occasions he wanted to interrupt the testimony of the teachers but Austin stopped him. When Fields was finally asked to make his comments he said that he would change, and in a dejected tone regretted the turn of events at the mission. He stated that the work he was doing at the mission was ultimately for the benefit of the African. These words turned out to be prescient for had Fields not pushed everyone to work hard, the mission could not have developed as it did.[44] Fields, in spite of his good intentions, was not sensitive to the needs and feelings of African workers under him. This seems to have been a common attitude among some early missionary leaders at Adventist missions. The cases involving Nyambo and Gudu and missionaries in chapters one and two, respectively, as has been shown, illustrate this problem.

---

[44] Interview, Matsimbe, 25 August 1998.

The African teachers' protest finally paid dividends. In his peroration, Austin announced that the protest was officially over. Fields was ordered to reinstate the teachers. A duty rota, clearly outlying the specific extra-curricular duties of each teacher, was drawn up. The heavy manual work was reduced. Teachers were given time to prepare lessons and attend to their family needs. Apart from this 'dent' on the history of the mission, the missionary era was better known for the industrial training school that symbolized the extent at which the mission had progressed under O.I. Fields.

Industrial Training School, 1953-1971

The idea to establish industrial schools in Unions in East and Central Africa was the brainchild of the EAD. In 1947, the EAD at its Bulawayo Council voted that in each Union, one school should be selected to offer industrial training courses primarily for sons of church workers not inclined to enter the teaching and evangelistic training. It should be observed that the Adventist church runs educational institutions primarily to provide the children of its members with an Adventist education. In Malawi, the Union chose Matandani mission to fulfil this purpose. For the Malawi Union, this could not have come at a more appropriate time. As earlier noted, the colonial government was becoming strict with the over-age policy. The government informed receiving schools that if they were to continue receiving the grant-in-aid the over-age policy was to be strictly adhered to.[45]

It should be noted that many students who were in mission schools were children of workers and to throw many of them out without offering them an alternative training would have seriously discouraged many faithful workers. Other factors were pertinent to the issue. S.G. Maxwell noted that "industrial training would also promote the church's teachings for a man with a trade could be independent in business and thus have

---

[45] In May 1955 the EAD's, executive committee decided to operate mission schools without government aid. Two reasons were cited for this move: first the fear that the church would eventually be prohibited to teach religious lessons in the schools and second the fear that energy and resources of the church would be used for purposes they were not originally meant for. See Bilima, "The SDA in Malawi", p. 66, 72.

no trouble in keeping the Sabbath."⁴⁶ Further, the Union observed that "many of the boys are very ambitious of furthering their education and learning some useful trade."⁴⁷ It was against this background that the idea of an industrial training school was a welcome development especially in Malawi.

The choice of Matandani mission to offer such courses was welcome news for O.I. Fields. As this section shows, Fields used the industrial training school to develop the infrastructure at the mission. In some cases, the mission won government contracts to roof or build houses. Through this, the school brought in money to the mission that was used to pay for operational costs. More importantly for the Malawi Union, a school like this was a pool for trained staff to work at its various missions especially at a time when the church was rapidly expanding and in need of new infrastructure. Towards the end of 1947, industrial classes were started at Matandani mission. The first courses offered were basic industrial skills subjects like bricklaying, carpentry, tailoring and tin smithing. Within a few years however, it became apparent that there was a need to upgrade these semi-skilled courses to more academic industrial courses. In 1953, the well-known industrial training school came into being when the semi-skilled courses were upgraded. The availability of electricity from 1956 onwards boosted the efficiency of teaching at the school because the heavy machinery used for practical lessons was now electrified.

By the end of the 1950s, the school began to attract not only students from Malawi but from other countries as well. Although many of the foreign students who attended the school were Adventists mostly sent by their home Unions, it is likely that the popularity of the school also attracted students who were not Adventists. The worldwide policy of the church on admission to its schools is that the SDA church does not discriminate in its admission policy. As long as the prospective student promises to respect the beliefs and practices of the church, admission is granted.

---

[46] Maxwell, *I Loved Africa*, p. 115. Note that SDA teaching on the Sabbath is that no temporal affairs shall be attended to except issues of faith and worship.

[47] EWEP "History of SEAU," p. 55.

The first courses that were offered at these levels were carpentry and joinery. The curriculum of these courses included the theory and practice of carpentry and mission work (two hours every day minimum for the latter). The period of study was four years, which was longer than at government technical schools. It is not clear from available sources why the length of time was extended but it would appear that there were advantages in this. Students gained valuable work experience especially in practical work before they graduated, a fact that made them more marketable than those who graduated from government run institutions with little hands on experience. The mission also seemed to have used this to its advantage because the industrial students helped in construction and repair work of mission's infrastructure. So, the longer they stayed at the mission, the more time was spent on mission projects. To find students with acceptable academic qualification to join the revamped training school was difficult at first. For example, only one student, W. Wingolo enrolled in 1953. The following year, two students, Sinapyanga (from Zambia) and M. Manyika,[48] enrolled.[49]

If the industrial training school was to attract students, further changes were necessary. By the start of the 1960s, new courses were introduced. Building and painting were added to the existing (carpentry and joinery) courses. Floods of students, both married and single from as far afield as Tanzania, Botswana, Zambia, Rwanda, Uganda and Zimbabwe came to attend the course. The exact numbers of foreign students and the countries they came from is difficult to ascertain from the sources available. Written sources[50] available show that these students came from Zambia, Tanzania, Botswana and Uganda while oral sources have added Congo, Rwanda, Kenya, Zimbabwe and Swaziland to that list. The

---

[48] M. Manyika joined Malamulo mission after completing his course and has been working there since. Interview, B. Thyoka, 26 August, 1998.

[49] Information from a logbook showing the names of all students enrolled in the industrial training school between 1953 and 1989. Kindly shown to the author by B. Thyoka, carpentry supervisor and former student of the Industrial Training School, Matandani Mission, 26 August 1998.

[50] The written sources here refer to the logbook noted above. This book has details on student enrollment between 1953 and 1989. This logbook shows the name of student, nationality, course undertaken, year of entry, year of exit and tools given.

student enrolment list in the appendix of this study is based on the written source.

So popular was the school at this time that many teachers in the primary school at the mission were attracted and joined the school. Boarding fee as from 1966 was 18 pounds. Students working on projects were paid 2/6 a day.[51] The first instructors at the school were Fields himself, Mr Gill and later a Mr Daniels. As the enrollment of students grew, more instructors were needed. To fill this gap, the mission began to use academically gifted students as assistant tutors. Many such students, upon graduation, were offered employment as instructors. The most noted of such student teachers included W. Wingolo, Sinapyanga, B.P. Makala, T. Chimwala and J. Mbuzi. To conform to government technical schools, the period of study at the school was later reduced first to three years, then to two and finally to one year.[52]

The need for trained industrial staff in the EAD became acute towards the end of the 1950s. The major reason for this need was the expansion of church infrastructure due to increased membership and increased enrollment in Adventist schools. It should also be remembered that it was during this time that indegenization was taking root throughout most of Africa and thus there was need for the church in Africa to have its own trained technical staff. Of all the industrial schools that were begun in various Unions in Africa per the recommendation of the Bulawayo council of 1947, Matandani Industrial Training School under the directorship of Fields was the most progressive. For this reason, the EAD voted that a maintenance course should be introduced at Matandani mission alongside the existing industrial school courses already taught at the school. In 1964, a two-year maintenance course through the initiative of the EAD was started at the mission. W. Duncan Eva, the secretary of the division stated, that "the purpose for which the course is being conducted

---

[51] MP Minutes of the Matandani Industrial School held at Blantyre on 22 December 1966.

[52] Interview, Thyoka, 24 August 1998 and interview, B.L. Chipazo, Matandani mission, 25th August 1998.

is to be able to provide for better trained men to care for the maintenance work at the larger institutions throughout the Division."[53]

Since the maintenance course was the brainchild of the EAD, students for the course were recommended by their respective Unions but approved by the Division. The employing organizations (i.e. the Unions) bore the financial costs of the student(s) they sent. The Division subsidized the operational costs through appropriation grants because the cost of training students was enormous. For example, tuition, books and laboratory fees amounted to 26 pounds. In addition, each student received a set of tools amounting to 48 pounds. In total, the sending Union spent 74 pounds per student.[54]

So popular was the new course that Unions in the EAD sent their students to attend the school. The maintenance course was an all-rounder. The subjects included general repairs, building, carpentry, maintaining industrial machinery, plumbing, electrical and industrial wiring. English, bible and industrial mathematics were offered as mandatory subjects. The maintenance programme was structured in a way that

> all students attend all classes but during the practical periods they are divided up into groups to practice those skills requested by the employing organization. For instance if a person, who is a qualified carpenter comes here, he attends all the classes including carpentry theory, but during the practical time, he does no carpentry, but learns something in which he is not qualified.[55]

Students in both the industrial and maintenance courses, especially those from Malawi, who wanted to obtain a national recognition, sat for the government trade test grades three, two or one after graduation. With the decline of appropriation or operational funds from the EAD to its institutions, Matandani mission could not afford to effectively offer both

---

[53] MP Letter from W. Duncan Eva, Secretary of the General Conference of Seventh-day Adventist Southern African Division to students (industrial and maintenance course), Matandani mission, 13 April 1964.

[54] Ibid.,

[55] MP "Matandani Training School." (a two page document with no author and no date).

the industrial and maintenance courses at the same time. As a solution, the two courses were merged into one and some of the subjects were dropped due to lack of instructors and equipment. The last students in the maintenance course graduated in 1970.

The Industrial Training School building

In all, by the end of the missionary era in 1971, 68 students had passed through the doors of the industrial training school. Two students who completed their course during the missionary era stand out. W. Wingolo (1953-1957),[56] one of the first students of the school, who also tutored briefly at the school, went on to set up a successful furniture business in Zingwangwa Township in Blantyre. W. Kamvayango (1955-1959) joined, upon the completion of the course, the now infamous Malawi Young Pioneers (MYP) and later became the Principal of Nasawa Technical School.[57]

---

[56] His son, Charles Wingolo, a graduate of Solusi University, is the current Treasurer of the Malawi Union (the first African in that post).

[57] The Malawi Young Pioneers (MYP) were an armed youth movement within the Malawi Congress Party (MCP) of the former dictator of Malawi, Hastings Kamuzu Banda. The powers of MYP superseded those of the national Police and Army. MYP reported directly to Kamuzu. The MYP could detect, detain and punish anyone who was suspected of opposing Banda and his

End of the Missionary Era, 1968-1971

O.I. Fields left Matandani mission on retirement in 1967 leaving a legacy that exists to this day. His achievements surpassed the efforts of many missionaries who worked at the mission. K.B. Cronje, Fields' replacement, begun his tenure as director in 1968. Cronje, who had been a missionary teacher at the mission before this appointment, was aware that if his tenure was to be remarkable his *modus operandi* as director was to differ markedly from that of Fields. One way he sought to do this was to concentrate on areas at the mission that Fields had largely neglected.

One such area was academic education. Since Fields' arrival in 1943 up until his departure in 1967, Matandani Mission School only offered primary school education at a time when secondary level education was much needed in Malawi. So, it became clear to Cronje that time was ripe for the mission to offer such type of education. After some consultation with the Malawi Union, Cronje submitted a proposal to Gwanda Chakwamba who was then Minister of Education seeking permission for the mission to open a junior secondary school.[58] The verbal response from the Ministry of Education was encouraging and based on that Cronje was hopeful that permission would be granted by the middle of 1968. Cronje went on furlough with the hope of finding a positive reply from the Ministry of Education on his return. However, when he returned in October 1968, the situation was not as he had expected. He went to Zomba, the then capital, to personally see the minister. The proposal was accepted and Cronje returned to Matandani mission triumphant.

---

government. Many people in the country were imprisoned, disappeared or were killed in this way. See Reuben M. Chirambo, "Politics in the Cartoon in Malawi: The Democrat Cartoons," in Kings M. Phiri and Kenneth R. Ross (eds.), *Democratization in Malawi: A Stocktaking*, Blantyre: CLAIM-Kachere, 1998, p. 205.

[58] Gwanda Chakwamba, a former cabinet minister in Banda's government is currently the president of the Malawi Congress Party (MCP), now the main opposition party in Malawi. Chakwamba is by church affiliation a Seventh-day Adventist having been converted and baptized in the church while serving a treason sentence imposed on him when he fell out of favour of the Kamuzu government.

In September 1969, history was made as the first form one students registered for formal classes. The pioneer African teacher of the school was Y. Mwandire, a Mang'anja by ethnicity, who come on transfer from Lunjika (formerly Mombera) Mission Secondary School in Mzimba. Mwandire taught mathematics and English at both the secondary and industrial schools. The other teachers were Cronje himself and his wife. Later, T. Nkungula and G. Kamwendo joined the teaching staff. One of the well-known students of this humble start is today Dr Mataya, who until his appointment in early 1999 to work at the GC, was the Medical Director of Blantyre Adventist Hospital. By the time Cronje left the mission for further studies in November 1970, the secondary school classroom-building proj??ect he had started in 1968 had been completed.[59] M.O. Klausen replaced Cronje in November 1970 but only stayed for four months. In April 1971, T. Nkungula became the first African to head Matandani mission, bringing the missionary era to its official close.

Even the camp meeting of 1969 reflected the coming of changed times at the mission. Two African pastors, Howa and Khwangwala, led this meeting. By the end of the camp meeting week, about 30 people were baptized by Pastor Khwangwala in the Nkulumadzi River. This meeting was also significant in some ways for it was the last centralized meeting for all churches under Matandani mission. In subsequent years and after the decentralization of many functions of missions in the country, members of Matandani church began to have their own camp meetings, a practice that continues to this day.

---

[59] Most of the historical account in this part of the discussion is based on the oral information of B Thyoka, interview, Matandani Mission, 25 August 1998.

Chapter 4

THE ERA OF NATIONAL LEADERSHIP 1971-1989

Rationale for Indigenization in the Adventist Church

Indigenization, the idea to have national workers run the affairs of local churches as opposed to missionaries, has been an initiative of the GC since the middle 1930s. When the Adventist church began its evangelical out-reach outside the United States in 1874 as already noted, a precedent had been started that continues to this day. With mostly American (and later British) missionaries in every field e.g. teaching, pastorate, administration and medical, the church has managed to spread the SDA message (i.e. the Three Angels' message and Sabbath worship) with much success. By the middle of the twentieth century, however, the church had started to replace missionaries with local staff to run the affairs of the church in foreign territories.

The starting point of this policy can be traced to the American depression of the 1930s.[1] In the early years of the church's history, tithe and donations from American members were the major source of income that was used to run the administration of the church and send out missionaries to foreign lands. Consequently, when the depression hit, the church suffered financially. Again, the expenses of many missionaries to foreign lands in those days were mostly met by family

---

[1] For detailed discussion of the effect of the depression on the SDA church, see D. Appel, "The Effect of the Depression on the SDA Church," term paper, Andrews University, USA (no date).

members and friends or well-wishers. As earlier noted for example, Ruth Konigmacher's father paid the sea fare to Africa for Samuel and Ruth.[2]

Apart from transportation and settling costs of the missionaries and their families, which the church had to pay for, there were other expenses as well that the church incurred. There were furlough travelling expenses for the missionaries and their families that the church was to meet. It was inevitable that if the church was to be financially secure in the troubled times of the depression, drastic measures to reduce operating costs were to be introduced. Even when the depression had passed, it was expensive to sustain a large missionary work force in foreign missions. One of the ways the church employed to save funds was to reduce the number of missionaries and increase the proportion of national workers in foreign missions. R.N. Schwarz contends that national leadership was the best solution because "these individuals proved less expensive to support. They needed no costly furloughs home and seemed willing, if not always completely content, to accept salaries substantially less than those paid to overseas missionaries."[3]

The Second World War (1939-1945) contributed in some ways to this change of policy. Not only did it become difficult to find missionaries willing to risk their life to travel to overseas missions at the height of the war, but also travelling restrictions imposed during the war compounded the situation. Therefore, the church had to elevate national workers to positions of responsibility to offset the lack of missionary workers. As it turned out, the pioneer national workers were not a let down. E.L. Longway, then president of the China Division, observed in 1946 that "every phase of the work has been fostered and kept intact."[4]

To a large degree, the rise of nationalism in Asia and Africa between the 1940s and 60s speeded up indigenization. With nationalism, there was a growing resentment among indigenous peoples against foreign domination and the exploitation of their territories and themselves. Unfortunately, missionaries, perhaps unaware of it, were themselves part

---

[2] Sandra Konigmacher, e-mail communication.
[3] Schwarz, *Light Bearers*, p. 573.
[4] Ibid.

of the total colonial culture of subjugation and exploitation.[5] With the talk of change everywhere in Asia and Africa, it was evident that local people were determined to free themselves from foreign domination. When most of the colonial territories began to attain their independence, it became imperative for the church to adjust to the changing times. Therefore, as colonial administrations were being taken over by local people, the Adventist church also began to rapidly replace the leadership of the church in these territories with local hands.

It should be noted that the Adventist church is not a proactive organization on social issues such as human rights, racism, gender, democracy etc. It would appear that its apolitical position prevents the church to speak up on such issues.[6] In this connection, the church is usually seen as one that only reacts to such issues as a secondary participant.[7] At best, the church is perceived by members and non members alike as one that is content with the political and social *status quo*. For example, during the era of institutionalized racism in both Zimbabwe and South Africa, the church not only kept silent about it but continued to allow its black and white members to hold separate church services. So deep was the racial problem in South Africa that when black and white Conferences and Fields in South Africa, Namibia, Lesotho and Swaziland were merged in 1991 under an African president, Douglas

---

[5] See Shepperson and Price, *Independent African*, p. 387. See also Klaus Fiedler, "Christian Missions and Western Colonialism: Soulmates or Antagonists?" in Kenneth Ross (ed.), *Faith at the Frontiers of Knowledge*, Blantyre: CLAIM-Kachere, 1998, p. 234.

[6] See Fiedler, '"Smaller' Churches and 'Big' Government," p. 168.

[7] It has been observed that the SDA church in Malawi usually addresses some issues based not on the theological teaching of the church but on what other Christian denominations do. For example, the policy to allow women to preach in SDA churches is based on the fact other churches are doing it. In a recent case, some members of Bangwe SDA church challenged the church to give biblical proof for this policy. These challenged the church administration to make policies based on Bible truth when dealing with religious issues and not on the fact that is the standard thing to do. The church administration reacted to this challenge by threatening these members with ex-communication. When the disagreement intensified, the church closed Bangwe SDA Church altogether. See Boyd Kazembe, "Bangwe SDA Church Closure Revisited," *The Nation*, 14 April 2000.

W.E.B. Chalale, to form the current Southern Union, the church attributed that possibility to nothing but to a miracle.[8]

During white rule in Zimbabwe, the racial problem was equally deep. There, if a black member went to Jamison (now Herbert Chitepo) SDA church, a "white" congregation in downtown Bulawayo city, the deacon on duty would "politely" inform the person that an "African" SDA church was nearby. The white deacon would go as far as giving detailed directions on how to get to the two nearby black churches of Makokoba and Pelandaba. Only when the political scene changed did black and white members began to freely attend the churches of their choice in Zimbabwe. In America, some African-American church workers voiced their concern over the church's reluctance to deal with the racial problem not only between black and white members but even in the policies of the GC that were prejudiced against black members.[9] Therefore, in some ways, the church appears to reinforce racist attitudes for its failure to condemn situations like those illustrated above. At Malamulo mission for example, there are two cemeteries, one for Malawian members and the other for missionaries.[10]

At the GC session of 1962, the church made the first admission that there is indeed racial prejudice against black people in the church. The GC president at the time, Reuben R. Figuhr promised that the church would look into the issue more critically with the view to eliminate racial prejudice in the church.[11] It would appear however, that very little was achieved in this regard. In 1975 Robert H. Pierson, then President of the GC, acknowledged that the church was doing little to address the problem. In his 254-page book titled, "We Still Believe" he encouraged racial equality of members within the church.[12]

---

[8] See Mathew Bediako, "Miracles in South Africa," *The Advent Review*, 6 February 1992, pp. 12-13.

[9] See *Insight Magazine*, 23 June 1990, p. 7.

[10] Note that until the late 1970s Malamulo Hospital had three types of hospital wards: One for Whites, another for Indians and yet another for Africans.

[11] Insight Magazine, p. 7.

[12] Quoted in Schwarz, *Light Bearers*, p. 627.

The church's policy on church and state relationship is an area where the church should be understood based on Adventist theological thinking and not in the conventional theological understanding. During the time of political transition (1993-1994) from dictatorship to democracy in Malawi, the church was silent at a time when most churches supported the movement for change. W.W. Masoka, then President of Seventh-day Adventists in Malawi summarized the church's position on matters of church and state. In the *New Express* of 11-17 June 1993, he stated that "our refusal to take part in party politics is not a lack of sympathy with the attainment of proper government, but it is due following the counsel of Christ that His 'kingdom is not of this world'."[13] While the church as an organization is apolitical, the policy on its members concerning politics appears paradoxical. According to Pastor Malopa, the current president of the church in Malawi, Seventh-day Adventists can join or support political parties of choice as long as the differing political views are not brought into the church![14]

Indigenization in Malawi coincided with the move to decentralize the administration of missions. In the early days, all institutions at a mission station were under the direct supervision of the mission director. For example, all missions in Malawi had at least a school, a church and a dispensary. As these mission institutions expanded, it became difficult for mission directors to effectively run them. One way employed to solve the problem was to declare some mission institutions to be Union institutions. Once an institution was declared a Union institution it reported directly to the Union. Unfortunately, when these changes were being made, the Union at the time did not make plain the reasons for decentralization. The result was that many local believers and some

---

[13] Quoted in Fiedler, "'Smaller Churches and "Big" Government," in Nzunda and Ross, *Church, Law and Political Transition in Malawi*," p. 166. Ken Bilima, the Director of Education in the Malawi Union stressed that the policy of the church is to co-operate with the government, preach love and stand for Jesus. Informal interview, Malawi Union Office, 23 April 1998.

[14] Informal interview, Pastor Malopa, Malawi Union President, Malawi Union Offices, Blantyre, 23 April 1998. Note that Elijah Mvundura, a Seventh-day Adventist theologian maintains that there can never be a union between church and state. See Elijah Mvundura, "Separation of Church and State: A Biblical Perspective (unpublished), 1999. (Draft document kindly provided to this writer by Mr Mvundura formerly from Zimbabwe but now living in Indiana, USA).

church workers held the erroneous opinion that these measures were done on racist grounds - that is; missionaries who had remained after indigenization did not want to be under African leadership.[15]

To illustrate this, the case of Malamulo mission is relevant.[16] Since its inception in 1902, the mission had been steadily expanding under a mission director. In 1948, the three major institutions of the mission (Press, Hospital and the Schools - primary and secondary) were declared Union institutions, each reporting directly to the Union. The Press was now under a general manager, the Hospital under a medical director and the Schools under a principal.[17] The perception of some local believers was that the Union, which was under a missionary president, was advocating these changes so that the medical director for the Hospital and the general manager for the Press (both missionaries) should not be under the supervision of an African director.[18]

This opinion persisted in spite of the important fact that the Malamulo schools continued to be administered by a missionary principal. It was not until 1972 that the first African principal for Malamulo schools, Pastor W.W. Khonje (1925-1997), was appointed.[19] Opinions like these which start with a rumour can be detrimental to the credibility of an organization like a church. What can be observed is that religious organizations are not open societies when it comes to how church policies are made and implemented. There is always secrecy about how things are done. While these policies are made in good faith and intended for a good cause, i.e. for the conversion of souls, the fact that members are left in the dark creates a breading ground for rumours. As has been shown above, some Adventist members were of the suspicion that the church was making

---

[15] Interview, S.F. Machilika, Matandani mission, 25 August 1998.

[16] From 1907 the mission was called Malamulo Training Institute. It trained primary and secondary students, hospital workers and pastors to certificate level and primary school teachers. In 1963, the mission was renamed Malamulo College. See MiP "Malamulo General School Prospectus," 1987/88, p. 2.

[17] EWEP "History of the SEAU," p. 53.

[18] Interview, Machilika, Matandani, 25 August 1999.

[19] The aspects on the personal life of Pastor Khonje were made available to the author by Mrs. G. Nzabonimpaye (daughter of Pastor Khonje), interview, Thamaga, Botswana, 9 April 1999.

these changes for racist reasons simply because the church administration did not openly inform its members about the rationale for these changes.

One of the disadvantages of indegenization was the reduction of financial support from the GC. Foreign[20] missions were now encouraged to find ways of finding their own sources of financial support. For foreign Unions, especially those in the developing world, it became particularly difficult to raise enough funds to sustain the operations of the church. In Malawi like in many African countries, the church was forced to advise its Union supervised schools (e.g. Malamulo, Matandani and Lunjika) to raise their operational funds through the collection of school fees. Matandani mission administration for example, has stressed that "the school is self supporting through its fees collection. The school however, accepts help from voluntary contributions and organizations."[21]

In spite of the problems that came along with it, indigenization was a welcome development, especially in Africa. The fact that African workers were allowed to run church affairs in their own countries, previously the domain of missionaries, was a step in the right direction.[22]

Triumphs of National Leadership, 1971-1989

Matandani mission was the first "big" Adventist mission in Malawi to be headed by a local administrator. The appointment of Tommy Nkungula[23] in 1971 was the fulfillment of the implementation drive for indegenization. Nkungula had been one of the first African teachers in the secondary

---

[20] The term "foreign" is used in this context to refer to any Adventist mission or Union outside the United States.

[21] MiP Matandani School Prospectus, 1998, p. 6.

[22] Gershon Amayo writing about the situation in Kenya observed that "the development of African leadership was encouraged by the appointment of Africans to the positions which were formerly dominated by Caucasians, such as station directors, field secretary-treasurers and presidents" (Gershom Amayo, "Seventh-day Adventist Contribution to Kenya," in Pfeiffer (ed.) *Seventh-day Adventist Contributions*, p. 61).

[23] With a doctorate in Education, Dr T. Nkungula who worked for many years as Education Director in the EAD is now a lecturer in the School of Education at Solusi University, Bulawayo, Zimbabwe.

school when it opened in 1969.[24] By the time Nkungula took over as mission principal, twelve missionary directors had been the directors of the institution between 1908 and 1971. Two of these, though temporary, were nationals. As already noted between 1917 and 1919, Kalinde Morrison Malinki and Moses Chauluka became the first African co-directors of the mission.[25] This appointment became possible because the church could not find missionaries who could come to Matandani as directors at the height of the First World War. For the same reason (i.e. lack of missionaries) Pastor Yokoniah Sosola was appointed full-time director in 1937, as which he served until 1938.[26] The appointments of these national workers as heads of the mission only lasted until missionary workers became available.

Nkungula became head of a mission that had fully functional primary and secondary schools. More significantly, as the previous chapter has shown, the mission boasted an industrial school that was the most popular in the whole division, especially in the 1960s and 70s. In fact, the industrial school enrollment for the school year 1970/71 was the highest in the history of the school. In this year thirteen students enrolled, including one from Botswana. This can be appreciated by observing that the average enrollment at the school was five per year.[27]

Nkungula did not make immediate major changes in the running of this relatively successful mission complete with a radio service.[28] In May 1971, a month before he was appointed principal, his predecessor, M.O. Klausen, had planned to introduce some changes to the structure of the

---

[24] Interview, B Thyoka, Matandani mission, 25 August 1998. In 1971 E.J. Zintambila was appointed as administrative secretary (second in command) of the Malawi Union. See *Seventh-day Adventist Yearbook* (1971), Washington: Review and Herald Publishing Association, pp. 257 and 266.

[25] See MiP Morrison Malinki, "The History of Pastor K.M. Malinki: An Autobiographical Sketch, (typescript).

[26] See MNA, "History of South East Africa Union," no author (typescript), pp. 42-43.

[27] See MP Logbook of student enrollment at Matandani Industrial School.

[28] In the early 1970s, the Radio Service was under the charge of a missionary named Hartley. By the late 1970s, the Radio Service had stopped functioning. See MP Minutes of Matandani Training School Board meeting held in Blantyre on 2 November 1971. Among other things, this meeting gave Mr Hartley permission in the unlimited use of the Radio Service.

industrial school. From 1964 up to 1970, the period of the industrial courses was two years. By the start of the indigenization era it was observed that most students did badly on the government trade test. One factor cited for this was that the two years of the course were inadequate to fully prepare students for trade tests. It was then decided to introduce a two-year supplementary course meant to prepare students for trade test grade three. But this decision was never implemented due to lack of resources and instructors. In fact, the reverse happened because the period of study was reduced to one year beginning in 1971 until the closure of the industrial school in 1989.[29]

However, by March 1971 some changes had been made to the curriculum of the industrial school courses. The syllabus was altered to give students as much theoretical and practical work as possible. For example, theory was extended from five to seven periods while practical work was extended from seven to fifteen periods per week. In addition to the core subjects, biblical teaching (Old Testament and New Testament studies), were introduced into the curriculum.[30] In June 1971, the Matandani Training School Board approved the incorporation of a brick-making course in the curriculum of the existing building course.[31]

Towards the end of 1973, Nkungula broke the *status quo* when he proposed the construction of the biggest project during his tenure. This was the proposal to build a girls hostel. Neither the mission nor the church had the money for such an undertaking. Nkungula approached the Beit Trust for financial assistance. Through its office in Zimbabwe, Beit Trust gave the mission K4500 to start the project.[32] Towards the end of 1975, Beit Trust made a further payment of K1125 as the last grant for the project.[33] Nkungula left for post-graduate studies in America at the

---

[29] MUMP Minutes of the special meeting to discuss the future of the Industrial School, 10 March 1971.

[30] Ibid.

[31] MP Minutes of the Matandani Training School Board meetings held at Matandani mission, 28 June 1972.

[32] MP Letter from H.P. Williams, Secretary of the Beit Trust, headquarters, England to Mr Nkungula, principal of Matandani Mission, 17 December 1973.

[33] MP Letter from J. H. Ingham, Beit Trust Representative in Rhodesia to the Principal, Matandani Training School, 4 October 1975.

end of 1975, before the hostel project was completed. A missionary O.R. Follet, who had been a science teacher in the secondary school, was appointed as principal. It should be observed that the appointment of Follet was because the church in Malawi did not have a qualified and experienced national to take over the running of the mission after Nkungula left.[34] Follet was to be one of the two missionary personnel to hold the position of principal during the indigenization era.

The start of 1976 saw further attempts to improve the quality of courses offered at the industrial school. In 1977, further courses such as agriculture, accountancy and typing were proposed to be included in the curriculum of the industrial school.[35] This proposal however was not implemented because of the continued lack of resources and staff. In the meantime, the girls hostel had been completed by the start of 1976. In his letter to the principal of Matandani mission, the Beit Trust representative in Zimbabwe, J.H. Igham, in a reply to a request by the mission to officially open the hostel wrote that the "opening of the girls hostel is scheduled for 30th June or 3rd July 1977. Colonel W.D. Lewis has been asked to open the building on behalf of Beit Trust."[36]

Another notable development during the indigenization era was the upgrading of the junior secondary school. In December 1980, a sub-committee was set up by the Malawi Union to study the feasibility of upgrading Matandani Junior Secondary School to form three and four to meet the demands as requested by the Traditional Authority and substantiation workers.[37] However, this proposal was only implemented thirteen years later when in January 1993, the junior secondary school was upgraded to offer form three and form four classes.[38] The secondary school continues to draw students from various parts of the country, both Adventist and non-Adventist.

---

[34] Interview, Machilika, 25 August 1998.

[35] MP Minutes of the South East Africa Union sub-Committee on Education: Goals and Objectives, 13 October 1977.

[36] MP Letter from J.H. Ingham, Beit Trust Representative in Rhodesia to the Principal of Matandani Training School, 17 May 1977.

[37] MP Minutes of the Matandani Training School Board, held in Blantyre, December 1980.

[38] MP Matandani School Prospectus (unpublished), 1998.

Adventist Churches in Neno: Weathering "Folk Churches"

The evangelical aspect of Matandani mission is one area that requires further research. Until recently, Matandani mission church and all its satellite churches could be described as folk churches. According to Klaus Fiedler, two types of churches may be found at a mission station. These are the "small gathered church" and the "folk church." Using the German Moravian missionaries in Tanzania as a case study, Fiedler found out that the intention of these missionaries "was not to establish a small gathered church but to establish a folk church." Fiedler admits that to define the concept folk church is difficult. In his attempts at its definition, however, he states that a folk church is one "which comprises a considerable part of or, ideally, the whole population of a given area and which relates positively to a people's cultural identity."[39]

This study suggests that Matandani mission church and its satellite churches (numbering 12 by 1923) befit the description of folk churches, a situation that also existed in villages where St. Armand Catholic mission had influence. In fact, in terms of religious influence, much of the Neno area was for a long time divided between Adventist and Catholic churches. Certain villages for example, were dominated by one of the two churches. To illustrate, villages such as Hira, Chidakwane, Kalimadzako and Masamba were "Catholic villages" while the rest of the villages around Matandani mission were "Adventist villages."[40]

In the "Adventist villages" oral accounts strongly indicate that people strictly observed Adventist practices like the observance of the Sabbath. After sunset on Fridays, for example, temporal activities were suspended until after sunset on Saturday. Beer drinking, polygamy and ancestral practices, things anathema to Adventists, were allegedly not common practices among Adventist members in these villages. There is a difference that should be noted between Klaus Fielder's case study and the one this study describes. While the Moravian missionaries

---

[39] Klaus Fiedler, Christianity and African Culture: Conservative German Protestant Missionaries in Tanzania 1900-1940, Blantyre: CLAIM-Kachere, 1999, pp. 37-38.

[40] Mrs. E. Nzume and M. Nzume, Samson village, 29 December 1999.

encouraged what today can be termed as "inculturation"[41] in their areas of influence, Adventist missionaries demanded that its converts abandon all "heathen" practices as a prerequisite for membership.

Map 3: Adventist Churches in the Matandani Mission Area

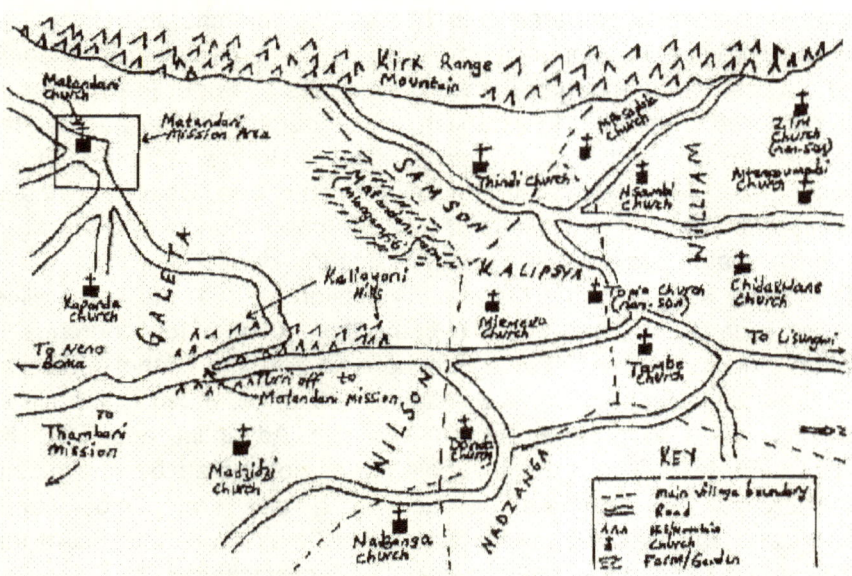

Over the years, some Adventist converts in the area have found it difficult to follow the strict teachings of the church. Many of these have succumbed to "unchristian" practices and vices such as polygamy and alcohol and this has led to their being expelled from the church. Unfortunately, many of those who backslide feel too shamed or are too proud to publicly confess, re-enter Bible class and receive a second

---

[41] The term inculturation could mean Christian worship and expression using people's traditional norms, instruments and catechetical creations. The Roman Catholic Church is at the head of this new movement. For aspects of a Catholic view on the subject, see Patrick Kalilombe, *Doing Theology at the Grassroots: Theological Essays from Malawi*, Gweru: Mambo, 1999, pp. 9, 30, 156, 163. See also Kenneth Ross (ed.), *Christianity in Malawi: A Source Book*, Gweru: Mambo, 1996, pp. 119-127.

THE ERA OF NATIONAL LEADERSHIP 1971 - 1989   115

baptism, the only course of action demanded from expelled members wanting to rejoin the church.[42] Not wanting this "humiliation", many of these people have left the church altogether. Another problem that has made some former SDA members in the area "disillusioned" with the church is the church's alleged failure to address people's social issues with the same enthusiasm it addresses spiritual ones. Unlike the Catholic Church and others in the area that sometimes distribute succor, clothing etc. when there is need, the SDA church is seen not to do the same.[43] Consequently, some members have left the Adventist church for a church that promises to provide such things.

Whether these are valid reasons to warrant a suggestion to the effect that Adventist churches in the area have lost their position as folk churches, will be clearly shown by further research. What has been observed however is that most Adventist churches in the area are no longer churches where "all" village residents are members and attend church services as a communal practice. There are some exceptions, however, where churches in some villages can still be described as folk churches. These villages are Nsambi and Manguo, where the Adventist Sabbath is still strictly observed. This is evidenced by the suspension of social and commercial activities in the villages at the approach of the "Sabbath hours" on Friday until the close of the Sabbath after sunset on Saturday.[44]

For much of the era of national leadership up to 1989, Pastor D.M. Masinga kept the spiritual aspect of the mission intact. In 1988 at an end of year board meeting he proudly announced that

> out of Bible class members, 17 were baptized during the last quarter. Second quarter 13 students were baptized. During June teachers' effort [week of evangelism conducted by teach-

---

[42] For aspects of the Adventist theology and practice on Rebaptism, see Matemba, "The Practice of Rebaptism in the SDA Church".

[43] Interview, Mrs. E. Nzume, Samson village, 28 December 1999 and Pastor Horace Nyirenda, Secondary school teacher, Matandani mission, 29 December 1999.

[44] Pastor Horace Nyirenda, 29 December 1999.

ers] 25 souls were won to Christ. In July 13 students were tl During the some time a ministerial club was started.[45]

Added to the "surviving" folk churches is of course Matandani mission church because all workers, students and villagers living in its vicinity congregate there. A clear indication that Adventist churches are no longer folk churches in many of the villages is the observation that today a number of different denominations have been established in the areas once a domain of Adventists. New churches that this study was able to identify include: Topia Church (TC), Zambezi Industrial Mission (ZIM), Assemblies of God (AG), Church of Central Africa Presbyterian (CCAP) and Mpingo wa Baptist (MwB).

From an initial observation, it appears that these new churches are attracting people, some former SDA members. In fact, churches like Topia accept polygamists and do not condemn beer drinking. Some former SDA members, who left the church because of such "sins", have joined Topia Church. However, it should be noted that Adventist churches are still in operation in the villages they were established (see map three above) notwithstanding the presence of these new churches and a perceived change in some people's attitude about the Adventist church.

Many Adventist churches in the Matandani mission area began as "companies".[46] These "small" congregations were formed through the efforts of Adventist evangelists and teachers from the mission. When out-schools run by missions like Matandani were taken over by government and given to district councils to run after the country's independence in 1964, Adventist evangelists continued to preach in the periphery of the mission. Through these efforts, prayer companies were established in many villages. For example, three of these companies: Kaliyoni, Kaponda and Kalitera later developed into churches.

The evangelical campaigns aided by the annual camp meetings at the mission, continued throughout the indigenization era. Teachers at the

---

[45] MUMP Minutes of Matandani Training School year-end board meeting, 8 November 1988.

[46] In the SDA church, a company, comprising a number of believers residing in close proximity to one another but not big enough to form a church, is the bottom institution in the church's organizational structure. After a company, there is the church, then the field, the conference, the union, the division and the GC. See *The Seventh-Day Adventist Church Manual*, p. 36.

mission school also contributed to the evangelical activities at the mission. These evangelized among their students with much success. Through these efforts many non-Adventist students, who attended any of the three schools (industrial, secondary and primary), were converted. Most principals at the mission, in spite of weaknesses in other areas, made great efforts to improve and deepen the spiritual dimension of the student body. For example, in 1989 the principal of the mission asked the Malawi Union to place the mission church pastor directly under mission control to enable the pastor to spend more time for internal evangelization (i.e. among the student body) as opposed to outside evangelism which seemed to take much of his time.[47]

If such positive pastoral developments had extended to the administrative realm, the mission could have continued to develop. However, sources show that the state of affairs at the mission in the years between 1977 and 1989 indicated that the mission was facing an uncertain future.

Impact of Indigenization, 1977-1989

Shepperson and Price in their poignant narrative of the John Chilembwe Rising of 1915 have warned that inevitability is a dangerous concept to use in a historical narrative.[48] For example, were the odds so against the national leadership in Malawi in general and Matandani mission in particular that mission establishments run by them were doomed to fail? Did the excitement of being in positions previously the domain of missionaries combined with less experience, training and the gradual reduction of financial appropriation from the GC, weigh too heavily for indigenous leadership to succeed? Were the dices too heavily loaded against Matandani mission indigenous leadership for it to save the mission from the rout that can be observed today?

Admittedly, several factors led to the decline of this mission in the indigenization era. Sources however indicate that the decline of the

---

[47] MUMP Matandani Training School Board of available members held in Blantyre on 27 October 1986. Note that when the administrative structure of the church was decentralized, churches were put under the direct control of Fields.

[48] See Shepperson and Price, *Independent African*, p. 339.

industrial school and its final closure in 1989 was one single indicator of the decline of the once admired Matandani mission. But there is another element that a historian should be cautious about in assessing the "pull" and "push" factors in a narrative. This is mono-causation. It would be misleading to attribute to a single factor the decline of a mission that by 1989 had been in existence for eighty-one years. It is the author's contention, based on observation, oral information and primary written sources that the decline of the mission, notwithstanding other factors, rests mainly on the decline and closure of the industrial school which in the writer's view was a "nail in the coffin" of the grandeur of the old Matandani mission.

Events at Matandani mission beginning from 1977 were perhaps a premonition of bad times ahead. The missionary Fischer replaced Follet as principal at the beginning of 1977. Fischer's tenure was brief due to his deportation by the Malawi government (MCP) over the Youth Week programme. In March every year in Malawi, during the Kamuzu Banda presidency (1964-1994), every institution and individual was expected to be actively involved in carrying out youth week activities. Anyone who did not take part in these activities was labeled a misfit of the Malawian society and the punishment of such an individual was always severe. For foreigners working in the country, the punishment was usually immediate deportation, a trend that continues today.[49]

In March 1977 the mission participated fully as had been the case in the past. Unfortunately, the last day of Youth Week for that year was on Saturday. The DC Mwanza sent a memorandum informing schools and institutions in the district and sub-district (in those days Neno was a sub-district) to be present at the closing ceremony. Fischer politely informed the DC that Matandani mission would not be present at the ceremony because the event fell on Saturday, a day strictly for worship for Seventh-day Adventists. The DC interpreted Fischer's failure to be present at the ceremony with students and staff as a sign of defiance of a government

---

[49] In 1998, the Malawi democratic government of Bakili Muluzi deported Max Church who was the Adventist Development and Relief Agency (ADRA) director, over comments he had made on the government's handling of non-governmental organization funding. Church was given the infamous twenty-four hour order to pack and leave the country. ADRA (Malawi), a branch of ADRA international, is an SDA organization concerned with relief matters.

directive. For this, Fischer was immediately given the infamous twenty-four hour order to leave the country.[50] He was to be the last missionary to work at Matandani mission.

The problem of the Sabbath has been a common occurrence in Malawi. During the presidency of Hastings Kamuzu Banda for example, Seventh-day Adventists were seen in a bad light because of their Sabbath observance.[51] Although the church is apolitical, it could not stop its female members to "dance for the Ngwazi" which they did, except on the Sabbath. Klaus Fiedler quoting a reader's comment in *The Nation* of 11-17 June 1994 states:

> Women members of the Seventh Day Adventist (sic) are the most hated under the current system because they refuse to go for dances on Saturday, (sic) We still call upon the MCP to respect the Sabbath and stop forcing women to attend to political matters on this day instead of worshiping God.[52]

For the SDA Church the Sabbath issue is actually a universal problem exacerbated by the church's strong evangelical piety and distinct theology.[53] In Kenya, Gershom Amayo observed that

> many more [Seventh-day Adventists] have been kept out of the mainstream of public life because of their firm stand on the observance of the Seventh-day Sabbath. A faithful Seventh-day Adventist would not accept any job which requires any work on the Sabbath day.[54]

The deportation of Fischer was perhaps a bad omen because by the beginning of 1977 signs of decline of the mission began to show. Due to

---

[50] Interview, Nzume, 24 August 1998.

[51] Dr Hastings Kamuzu Banda (1898-1997) was the first president of the Republic of Malawi. His despotic rule however, was infamous for abuse of human rights and for political oppression. See *Pride* Magazine (second edition), 1999, pp. 15-39.

[52] Klaus Fiedler, "The 'Smaller' Churches and 'Big' Government," in Nzunda and Ross, *Church, Law and Political Transition in Malawi*, p. 168.

[53] Ibid.

[54] Amayo, "Seventh-day Adventist Contribution," p. 65.

Fischer's untimely departure, Pastor Mambala was asked to manage affairs until a replacement principal was appointed. In May 1977, Pastor M.T. Kachoka was appointed acting principal. The financial situation at the mission was weak when Kachoka came. In an attempt to salvage the situation, he decided to downsize staff. In a memo to Pastor D.M. Masinga, the assistant deputy principal and the mission's church pastor, he stated that "as from 1 August 1977 some of the labourers will stop working and others will have their salaries revised. Others like Mr W. Lukiasi will be given K8, his six months salary to quit in December."[55] It is evident that by 1977 desperate measures were to be adopted if the mission was to stay afloat. But was the laying-off of low-level type of workers a solution to a problem that threatened the existence of the entire mission? Couldn't have the mission administration tried to find the real cause of the financial woes instead of victimizing people who were not responsible for the poor policies that had weakened the mission financially?[56]

Towards the end of 1977, Pastor W.W. Khonje came to Matandani mission as principal. Pastor Khonje had been the principal of Lunjika mission in Mzimba prior to coming to Matandani. Trained as a teacher and later ordained as a pastor, Khonje was the embodiment of a successful Adventist African worker in post-colonial Malawi.[57] In spite of his brilliance and excellence in the pastorate, Khonje's style of leadership was insufficient to salvage the deteriorating standards and financial woes at Matandani.[58] He was the office type of administrator who took little

---

[55] MP Internal memo from the Deputy Principal, M.J. Kachoka to the Assistant Deputy Principal, Pastor D.M. Masinga, July 1977,

[56] At the last research visit for this study between 28 and 29 December 1999 the author observed that some of the low level type of workers were laid off and the reason given was that the mission was facing a financial crisis. Manuel Nzume, one of the oral informants of this study, who during the author's first research trip in August 1998 was the mission's messenger, is one of those who has been laid off.

[57] It was common in the SDA church to ordain church workers of strong repute but who had never received theological training. Pastor Khonje was one such person. , Mrs. Nzabonimpaye.

[58] As a student, he wrote one of the best Cambridge papers in Malawi in the 1950s. See Josephine C. Edwards, "Graduation at Malamulo," *The Youth's Instructor*, 2 October 1951, p. 10.

interest to physically check what was going on outside his office at the mission. Seeing the new principal's *modus operandi*, casual workers and others took advantage of this weakness on the part of the new principal. Cases of truancy and work inefficiency increased.[59] By the time he was transferred in 1978 to work at the Union office, Matandani mission had regressed. The case of Pastor Khonje is not unique in the church. Appointments to administrative responsibilities in the church are usually based on one's merit as a pastor. The more successful one is as a pastor, the more are the chances that that individual will be given a post of responsibility. At Matandani mission, many pastor-administrators in spite of their dedication lacked the administrative skills and experience to head such an institution.

Pastor M. Sosola (the son of Pastor Yokoniah Sosola) was appointed acting principal when Pastor Khonje left in 1978. Later, he was confirmed principal of the mission. His tenure like that of Pastor Khonje's was largely uneventful. In 1984, E.G. Kamwendo replaced Sosola and the real problems of indigenization that had been building up over several years came to the fore. The 1985/86 financial year showed how grave the situation was. The school farm, due to careless supervision, did not make any profit. The tractor that at times was hired out to make extra-income for the mission had been involved in an accident with the principal and thus could not be used.[60]

Natural phenomena also played part in the problems of the mission at this time. The heavy rains of 1985/86 destroyed some mission infrastructure, and money not budgeted for such eventualities was used to repair the damage. The heavy rains destroyed the farm at the mission and this resulted in the loss of yield that year. The rains also destroyed part of the hydroelectric canal and this led to an interruption of electricity resulting in the stoppage of work at the industrial school. Since the industrial machines could not work, the carpentry unit could not make furniture for sale. The electric maize mill at the mission that also supplied money for

---

[59] Interview, M. Nzume, 24 August 1998.

[60] MP Matandani Training School memo from the Principal to the Deputy Principal on the 1985/86 unusually large expenses at Matandani mission.

operational expenses could not function because of the interruption of electricity.[61]

Coinciding with the unusually large expenses incurred in the 1985/86 year was also the loss of the yearly operational grant from the Union. Since the advent of indigenization, the GC had gradually begun to reduce its operational grants to Divisions and Unions. Inevitably, foreign missions had to be financially independent by relying on members' tithe. Even at Union level, the church could not rely on tithe revenue alone to provide for operational funds for its institutions. So, all Union institutions in Malawi had to raise their own funds by charging customers more for the services they sought. At Matandani, fees for the primary, secondary and industrial schools were the only source of steady income.[62] The danger with this was that if the schools could not attract enough students, the mission could easily face closure.

So, Matandani mission like other missions in the country was expected to raise money from student fees, a situation that continues to this day. However, in spite of the untiring efforts of the successive principals at the mission, raising enough money through fees became a *herculean* task. The lack of money at Matandani mission meant that the existing infrastructure could not be properly maintained. New projects to build or replace invalid infrastructure could not be undertaken unless the mission found a donor to sponsor a specific project.[63] One major problem that indigenous leadership faced at Matandani mission was that they could not easily attract funding for projects from American or European Adventist sources. The reason seems to have been that there was little trust by such donors to provide large sums of money for projects at the mission. The missionary leadership, it should pointed out, did not get most of its funding from church sources but from acquaintances and well-wishers back home. Indigenous leadership could not tap this source of income because they were unknown and often not trusted.[64]

---

[61] Ibid.

[62] , Machilika 25 August 1998.

[63] Currently at the mission, there is a building project of a dinning hall and a library sponsored by ADRA (Malawi).

[64] , Machilika, 25 August 1998.

Towards the end of 1986, the maize mills on the outskirts of the mission began to break down. The first to break down was the mill at Nchawe and then the one at Mitumbu followed. The mill engines were brought to the mission for repairs but due to lack of money to buy spare parts, the engines were left unattended to for many years. Later, the engines were broken apart and the parts sold.[65] In 1987, a year before he left Matandani mission, E.G. Kamwendo was part of a board meeting that convened to find ways of salvaging the industrial school which was under the threat of closure if no drastic measures were taken. This meeting resolved to ask the school administration to write letters to church leaders in the entire Union to help recruit students for the school. In fact, it was decided to send a plea for finance and student enrollment through the Union's local publications for example, *Outlook*, *Tidings* and *Ministerial Exchange*.[66] By the time E.G. Kamwendo left the mission in late March 1987 for post-graduate studies in the Philippines, the situation relating to finance and poor student enrollment had not improved.

After E.G. Kamwendo left, G.H. Kunkhoma, who had been the mission's registrar, was appointed acting principal and would serve in that capacity until his early death in April 1988. During his tenure as principal, Kunkhoma observed that most of the existing mission infrastructure was in poor state and needed urgent repair. He also noticed that while enrollment in the secondary school was good, examination results were not. Financially, too, the mission had not improved. In a desperate attempt, once again, it was decided to lay off many general workers.[67] It is evident that Kunkhoma took over a mission that was reeling with problems that had accumulated over several years. The death of Kunkhoma created further problems because the Malawi Union struggled to find a replacement and for a year the mission stayed without an effective principal.

---

[65] Nzume, 25 August 1998.

[66] MUMP Matandani Training School Board of available members held in Blantyre on 27 October 1986.

[67] MUMP Matandani Training School Board minutes of year-end meeting, 9 December 1987.

On 1 April 1988, a few weeks before Kunkhoma died, E.Y. Ntata, who had been a teacher at the mission, was appointed acting registrar.[68] When the principal fell ill and died as already noted, Ntata was asked by the church to act as principal, a responsibility he reluctantly accepted. The inability of Ntata to effectively manage affairs at the mission compounded the already deteriorating situation at Matandani. This situation compelled the church to actually propose that "since the grave problems of the institution have been due to lack of skilled and dynamic leadership, it was voted that Dr Nkungula and a missionary volunteer be called to go and work at Matandani with effect from 1 January 1989."[69]

This decision by the Union begs the question: Was this a reversal of the indigenization drive and a return to the 'good' old days? Was the Matandani mission board's decision an admission that the mission needed missionaries to bring it on its feet again? Dr Nkungula, the pioneer African principal at the mission, who by then was the education director in the EAD, declined the 'call' to go to Matandani. Even the appeals for a missionary volunteer did not attract a positive response. A frantic search for a principal for Matandani mission by the Malawi Union Education Director was launched. At Matandani, E. Ntata had already submitted his letter of resignation and was waiting for the next principal to come and relieve him of his duties. In April 1989, B.D. Kadzombe who had been teaching at Blantyre Commercial Private School in Blantyre accepted a 'call' to work for the church as the new principal of Matandani mission.[70]

B.D. Kadzombe found Matandani mission on the brink of financial collapse, a consequence of many years of poor management. The hydroelectric canal and the engine for the hydroelectric plant badly needed repairs. The maize mills had broken down and enrollment in the industrial school was at its lowest in its 36 years of existence. Although Kadzombe tried his best to keep the mission from rout, he was fighting

---

[68] See MUMP Minutes of Matandani Training School on campus mid-year board meeting, 29 March 1988.

[69] MUMP Minutes of Matandani Training School year-end board meeting, 8 November 1988.

[70] Informal interview, B.D. Kadzombe, former Principal of Matandani mission and now a teacher at Malamulo Secondary School, Blantyre, 31 December 1998.

against a 'current' that had been building up over many years since the era of indigenization began. Other Christian churches in Malawi undergoing leadership change from missionary to local also experienced similar problems. Silas Ncozana has noted that at Blantyre Mission of the Church of Central Africa Presbyterian (CCAP) "the legacy of huge mission stations built by missionaries, now left without funds for maintenance, was a financial burden on the young leadership."[71] In 1989, two weeks before Kadzombe became principal, the famous industrial training school at Matandani, closed its doors, signalling in the researcher's view the 'official' decline of the mission.

Events that led to the closure to the industrial school can be traced to 1967 when its pioneer, O.I. Fields, left on retirement. The school had progressed because of the personal efforts of Fields. Although several missionaries came after him, they did not have the same enthusiasm and dedication. The coming of indigenization in the 1970s added salt to injury and it appears that it was just a matter of time before all hell would break loose. In 1980, new hopes were raised with the appointment of the first Malawi Union African President, F. Botomani (1926-1998), whom people thought would help solve the problems that were at Matandani mission. Members' expectations were further raised for it was assumed that with his connections with high-ranking church officials at the EAD (where he had been working) and the GC he would be able to attract the necessary funds not only for Matandani mission but for other missions in the country as well.[72] However, this was not to be the case.

By 1980, all staff at the mission was local. In the industrial school most of the staff was made up of former students of the school. The 1979/80 mission prospectus shows that the staff in this school included: M.L. Mtambo as head of the school, B.P. Makala in-charge of carpentry and joinery, F.G. Nkhoma head of the bricklaying unit and S.J. Tsoka in-charge of auto-mechanics.[73] Sadly, the indigenous euphoria at

---

[71] Ncozana, *Sangaya*, p. 35.

[72] Before his appointment as Malawi Union's first national President, Pastor Botomani had been a field secretary at the EAD headquarters in Harare, Zimbabwe.

[73] MP Matandani Mission Prospectus, 1979/80. Note that all these people were former students of the Industrial school.

Matandani mission was short-lived. In a few years, it became evident that the industrial school had little chance of overcoming the many hurdles in its way.

In 1982, the mission reported that auto-mechanics was cancelled from its curriculum due to lack of staff and equipment. The performance of the carpentry and joinery and bricklaying students in the trade test was also an indicator of the declining state of the school. The trade test results released on 5 August 1982 showed that of the four students who sat for grade three trade test in carpentry and joinery, only two passed. In the same year, ten students sat for bricklaying trade test grade three and only four students passed.[74] By 1985, the situation had remained the same. The total pass percentage of the trade test grade three for both bricklaying and carpentry and joinery was 57.[75]

In April 1986, suggestions were made to upgrade the industrial school in order to prepare students for trade test grade two.[76] But this turned out to be wishful thinking because the school lacked instructors. M.L. Mtambo, who headed the school for sometime, left in September 1986. The mission asked B.L. Makala to act as head of the school so that the school could prepare for the 1986/87 school year.[77] It was now clear that if no drastic changes were made in the running of the industrial school, its future was doomed. Other factors contributed to the situation. The decline of appropriation to missions as earlier noted drastically affected the school. The industrial school, which had a large operating expenditure, had to depend on students' fees to remain in full operation at a time when student enrollment had considerably declined. By 1980, the mission administration had begun to complain to the Malawi Union that student fees and workshop sales were not enough to meet the financial obligations of the industrial school and the entire mission.[78]

---

[74] MP Letter from the Ministry of Labour, Superintendent of Trade Test to the Principal, Matandani Training School, 5 August 1982.

[75] MP Matandani Training School Examination results for 1985.

[76] MP Minutes of the Matandani Training on-campus Board held at Matandani on 3 April 1986.

[77] MP Letter from the Principal, H.G. Kamwendo, Matandani mission to the Education Director, South East Africa Union, 25 September 1986.

[78] Thyoka.

Further woes awaited the school. The industrial school began experiencing a serious shortage of instructors. Reacting to this shortage, the mission began to use final year students and those who had just completed their course to work as instructors. Many of these were either ill-qualified or lacked the necessary experience to meet the teaching needs of the students at the school. Soon, students began to complain about the incompetence of such instructors in the school. One instructor who faced an open complaint from students was J. Kabambe who had come in to help students prepare for their trade test as there was no instructor available.[79] In an attempt to acquire instructors for the school, the Malawi Union sent Dan Msowoya[80] and later J. Kabambe to the University of Eastern Africa (Baraton) in Kenya for degree courses in industrial technology.[81] However, by the time these two finished, the industrial school had been closed.

The lack of tools for practical examinations made worse, *inter alia*, by student theft, brought further problems to the industrial school. Completing students who were given toolboxes for use during their trade tests in Blantyre did most of the theft. As it often happened, the students never returned the toolboxes to the school after the examinations. Worse was the fact there seemed to be no mechanisms put in place by the mission to contain the situation. So acute was the lack of tools for the school that during practical lessons students had to queue for tools. In January 1985 Principal E.G. Kamwendo appealed for financial support of K5257 from the Adventist Relief Agency (ADRA) at the EAD to purchase equipment and books.[82]

---

[79] Ibid.

[80] Today, Dan Msowoya is the publicity secretary of the opposition political party called Alliance for Democracy (AFORD). Msowoya severed ties with the church after a disagreement over work related issues. He had been working as workshop manager for Blantyre Adventist Hospital in Kabula, Blantyre before he left church employment.

[81] University of Eastern Africa (Baraton) is a Seventh-day Adventist University located in Eldoret in Kenya. The land where the university is built, was given to the SDA church by the President of Kenya, Daniel arap Moi.

[82] MP Letter from the Principal Matandani Training School E.G. Kamwendo to C. Patterson, Director of ADRA Department, Eastern Africa Division, Harare, 17 January 1985.

By the start of 1989 it was clear that the industrial school was a 'sinking ship' and very little could be done to save it. The Malawi Union set up a committee to look into the affairs of the school. The committee was made up of E.Y. Ntata, B.D. Kadzombe, J.H. Kanjira, G.S. Moyo[83] and D. Kasoti. At the meeting of 3 April of that year, the committee noted that the turnover from the industrial school was too low to support the school. Two factors for this were cited: poor enrollment and low tuition fees. The committee noted that the school had a long and outstanding historical background and efforts were to be made to save it at all cost. Two suggestions were made in this attempt. First, the fee structure was to be re-studied and appropriate recommendations made. Second, the instructors in the school namely: Mletseni, Makala and Nkhoma were to be reprimanded in connection with the declining standards in the school. It was decided that this task be undertaken by three people: the Union President, Union Secretary and Matandani Principal.[84]

The committee did not see its suggestions implemented. Two weeks after submitting its report and recommendations to the Union, a sub-committee on the future of the industrial school was hastily set up by the Union. This committee recommended to the church that the school could not be saved and had to be closed down. This special committee felt that the financial position of the school did not warrant the mission to continue the operation of the school. Finally, the committee voted "to recommend that the Industrial School be closed or suspended for one or two years until the financial position is improved. But voted that the school operate (sic) carpentry shop only."[85] A few days after this recommendation was made, the chairman of the Matandani Training School Board, F. Botomani, in his capacity as the President of the Malawi Union, came to the mission with a solemn message. In the

---

[83] G.S. Moyo was the most successful national principal of Malamulo and later Lunjika secondary schools. He is at present (2000) the Registrar of the University of Eastern Africa, Baraton, Kenya.

[84] MUMP Minutes of Matandani Training School on campus Board meeting held on 3 April 1989.

[85] MUMP Minutes of a meeting of the sub-committee on the future of Matandani Training School held in Blantyre on 17 April 1989.

hearing of both students and staff of all the institutions of the mission, he announced that the industrial training school was to be closed down temporarily due to circumstances beyond control.[86]

The school has not been reopened and its buildings and equipment lay neglected. Apart from the closure of the industrial school, the breaking down of the hydroelectric plant and other visible signs of decline that can be observed at the mission, the secondary and primary schools, the dispensary and more importantly, the church are still in operation. The mission continues its evangelical work especially among the students at the mission. The further decentralization of the administration of missions in Malawi has limited the evangelical scope of missions like Matandani. Today, there is no church in Malawi that is under the direct control of a mission because that function is now the responsibility of Fields. There are three Fields in the administrative organization of the church in Malawi. These are: South Malawi Field, Central Malawi Field and North Malawi Field. Each Field is under a Field President who reports directly to the President of the Malawi Union at the church's headquarters in Blantyre. A Field is made up of districts and each district is under a district pastor who is responsible for the evangelical work in that district.[87]

As can be seen, most of the evangelical functions that the Matandani mission church pastor used to perform, have now been taken over by the district pastor. Today, the target for much of the evangelical work by the Matandani mission church pastor and teachers are the non-Adventist students who come to attend both the primary and secondary schools. The continued popularity of the schools in attracting boys and girls, who

---

[86] Interview, B. Thyoka, 25 August 1999.

[87] See Yonah H. Matemba, "Aspects of Seventh-day Adventist Church Polity: The Case of the Malawi Union," (unpublished) post-graduate module paper, University of Malawi, Department of Theology and Religious Studies, May 1998, p. 4.

come to attend this unique Adventist education, far away from the influence of cities, has remained one of the ways in which Matandani mission continues to contribute to the conversion of people into the Adventist church.

CONCLUSION

Matandani mission, unlike its contemporary Malamulo, was founded because people in the area wanted the church to come there. While missionaries eventually came and built up the mission, African workers helped them in their work. The pioneering work of Mark Chakachadza in the founding of Matandani mission proves the African role in the establishment of Christian missions in Africa. Although it would appear that after the mission was established Chakachadza's prominence waned, the school that he started survived until the time of independence in 1964. Why Chakachadza's activities are largely unknown after 1908 is something that this study failed to establish. What only appears to be remembered of his achievements even by his grand daughter is that he brought the SDA church to Matandani. Perhaps that is how we should remember him.

The pioneering work of Peter Nyambo at Matandani mission was until now unknown. In fact, Nyambo worked longer at Matandani than at Malamulo mission. He worked for a few months at Malamulo towards the end of 1907 and part of early 1908. From 1908 until he left the church in 1911, he was at Matandani mission. Nyambo, it should be noted, was the first African to work as an assistant to a missionary at both Malamulo and Matandani missions, an achievement that was not repeated until the era of indegenization. Surely, his work and activities in the Adventist church should be re-examined.

The work and sacrifice of pioneer missionaries is equally important to the story of Matandani. Up to this day, the Neno area is still covered with thick forests. To imagine these missionaries coming to the area before 1950 was a sure sign of their dedication and zeal in the propagation of Christian work. Oral accounts at the mission indicate that on many occasions missionaries had to use their guns to drive away wild animals around the mission. Although some like Fields at times overstepped their boundaries, missionary contribution to the development of the mission was invaluable. The death of children and spouses and burying them so far away from home could have dampened the spirits of even the strongest person. Nevertheless, missionaries like Konigmacher and Davy accepted such tragedies as worthy scarifies to the work God had commissioned them to do.

The history of the Adventist church until the beginning of the 1920s is concentrated on Malamulo and Matandani missions. Small wonder then that most of the pioneer African workers worked at both missions. This explains the reason why both missions were alleged to have assisted directly or indirectly in the Chilembwe Rising. Although there were other general issues to the suspicions as noted in the study, all the prominent people named by government: Philip Chinyama, Morrison Malinki and Peter Nyambo had worked at both missions. More important is the fact that these African workers had close associations with Joseph Booth, a missionary whose good intentions had unintended results like the Chilembwe Rising and the general rise of independency in Malawi.

The success of the mission (until early 1970s) should be attributed to the combined efforts of both African and missionary workers. While most administrative responsibilities were confined in the hands of missionaries mainly because of the colonial attitude of the time, it is evident that the African contribution especially in the establishment of schools and churches in the surrounding areas was immense. Missionaries themselves admitted that in the outlying areas, the African contribution was unsurpassed. Unknown to missionaries, this hard work by local workers had unforeseen consequences. Since they were working hard, they expected something in return, a promotion, raise in salary or an acknowledgement. When missionaries ignored this, there were problems as the case of Nyambo has shown. We can even trace the source of some of the "anti-missionary" attitude of Gudu and the leaders of the teacher's protest of 1953, to this.

We have seen from the discussion in the study that there was a shortage of missionaries to go round in the early years of Adventist work in Malawi. The employing of former missionary children, themselves hardly experienced to handle the daunting task of missionary

CONCLUSION 133

responsibilities was a clear sign of this problem. Another example was the recalling of missionaries who had earlier been at the mission as the cases of L. Davy and G.A. Ellingworth have shown.

Three African workers, M. Chauluka, M. Malinki and Y. Sosola were at some point (during the missionary era) given the overall responsibility to administer the mission as directors. Clearly, these appointments were by default. The impression given that the Adventist church was ready to relinquish, willingly, the administration of its missions to Africans at this early stage of the church's existence in Malawi, is a false one. This can be illustrated by observing that it was only when the church did not have missionaries to head the mission that Africans were allowed to manage affairs at the mission, only to be sidelined when a missionary worker came. A bonus point for African leadership at the mission should be mentioned. Although it can be argued that the period they worked as directors was short and thus insufficient to make valid conclusions, it is worth to note that not once did it happen that during their leadership the mission faltered. Either they maintained the *status quo* or work progressed. Klaus Fiedler in his historical analysis of Faith Missions has stated that

> within a century, Africa South of the Sahara has changed its religion and has become a Christian continent. The enormous evangelistic effort that was required for this process of change was initiated by European and US missionaries, but the *biggest amount of work* was done by Africans, whether through informal witness to their new-found faith or through part-time or full-time service of the emerging church as teachers, evangelists or (later) as pastors[1] (emphasis supplied).

The significance of the protest of Wilfred Gudu at Matandani mission between 1922 and 1925 should be noted. The reason is that this was the first example of serious internal dissatisfaction by African workers who were unhappy with the way missionaries, at times, dealt with them. Not wanting to keep quiet or silently quitting like the teachers at Malamulo, as

---

[1] Klaus Fiedler, *The Story of Faith Missions*, Oxford: Regnum, 1994, p. 364.

the study has noted, Gudu did the unthinkable at the time by openly speaking out. This study has shown that the problem between Gudu and the Adventist church begun at Matandani and not at Malamulo mission as other studies on the subject have indicated. By bringing in a fresh reconstruction of the genesis of the squabbles between Gudu and the church, the study has further challenged the chronological account of this story in existing literature.

The study has outlined the side of the history of Matandani mission until now not properly investigated. Except the impact of the Chilembwe Rising and partly the Gudu Affair, the African teachers' protest has remained a "hidden" historical development in the Adventist church in Malawi. The significance of such protests to a church that prides itself of having a distinct piety is that the Matandani mission story, like stories of most Christian missions in Malawi, had both "smooth" and "rugged" times.

Indigenization in the Adventist church did not come as a result of a deliberate policy to hand over church leadership to national workers but as a compromise to an existing situation, a common practice in the church. As a consequence, the church hastily handed over work to workers who were by and large ill prepared for such a role. As has been shown in this presentation, most of the indigenous workers who took over the reigns of leadership lacked the skill to propell the mission into further development. One factor that contributed to this problem was the frequency of replacement of national principals at the mission. For example between 1908 and 1977, the mission had thirteen missionary directors compared to six African principals between 1971 and 1989. This could as well explain why during the indigenization era, there was little progress because there was lack of continuity. A few months, one year or two years were inadequate for a principal to fully implement his plans for the mission. It should be noted that the missionary O.I. Fields did so much because he was at the mission for twenty-four years. The frequency also indicated the loss of confidence (by the Malawi Union) in the administrative abilities of many of the principals.

Ultimately, the blame for the general decline of the mission lies with the Malawi Union. While the office was best at replacing mediocre principals, it failed to monitor closely what the principals at the mission were doing. Had this happened, the industrial school might not have been closed because the problems associated with it could have been noted before they became difficult to handle. While African instructors in the school did their best, they seemed to have lacked the necessary industrial experience and skill to run the school. This raises the question: could the school have survived had missionary instructors been retained? The policy of the GC to reduce appropriation to its foreign missions was a suicidal move. In areas like Malawi where the general membership is largely poor due to the economic situation of the country, the little tithe and donations collected are not enough to sustain the needs of a growing church and its institutions. Consequently, the church was compelled to advise missions to find their own sources of income. At Matandani and indeed at all Adventist missions in the country, this proved to be difficult for missions to do. The result was a steady decline in the standard of services provided by these missions. With the general decline of income for the majority of Malawians who send their children to private schools like Matandani, the decline of enrollment meant a loss of revenue.

The financial situation at the mission was worsened by the inability of indigenous leadership to find alternative sources of income. Relying mainly on student fees was suicidal for the existence of the mission. There could have been deliberate efforts to make use of the large farm the mission has to grow different kinds of crops for sale. The maize mills should have been maintained or revived. Mission work should have been used wisely to minimize operational costs on casual labour. The history of Matandani mission is ironical. While it were the indigenous people that initiated its founding and helped in its development, they were also the ones that contributed to its regression.

Sadly, the general infrastructural decline at Matandani mission is evident at most Adventist missions in the country and indeed in Africa as a whole.[2] George Mwansa, a Seventh-day Adventist pastor and editor of the EAD newspaper called *Outlook* has noted that

---

[2] For example, Chinyama mission in Mulanje, Thekerani mission in Thyolo and Chileka mission in Blantyre have, a part from the churches that exist today, little mark showing that in the 1940s and 1950s these were vibrant SDA missions complete with schools, dispensaries and houses for mission workers.

while building new structures is important, maintaining them is another. Many immaculate structures put up some years back have undergone a kind of metamorphosis that leaves much to be desired. Leaking roofs, rusty doorframes, soiled ceiling boards and walls that have long lost their colour not to mention the antiquated furniture are a common sight in many denominational institutions.[3]

Whether this is a sign that indigenization has failed to deliver, is a subject that future research will reveal. What this study has found out at this stage is that with indigenization local workers alone have found it very difficult to maintain the same standard that Adventist missions were famous for during the time of the missionaries. While it can be argued that missionaries had much support (financial and otherwise) from the GC, it is a challenge that the Malawi Union leadership should objectively deal with in order to find ways of raising money to manage and maintain the church's institutions. If no constructive decisions are implemented urgently, many of the church's institutions will surely close down. Perhaps what the Malawi Union lacks is not so much loads of money but what Armando Lopez, the former Treasurer of the Zimbabwe Union Conference, calls philosophy[4] – that is if the Malawi Union wants to bring back quality to its institutions it can do it. It is a question of commitment.

---

[3] George Mwansa, "Zimbabwe Union Conference: A Pride of Eastern Africa Division," *Outlook*, volume. 17, number 3, July-September 1999, p. 20.

[4] Ibid.

APPENDICES

i. Notes on Notable Oral Informants

(a). F. L. Matsimbe

Born in 1911 he came to Matandani mission between 1922 and 1923. He attended his early primary school there and in 1928 went to Malamulo mission to do his standard 5 education. He went to Zimbabwe soon after Malamulo and came back in 1950. A year later he joined Matandani teaching staff. He was an active participant in the strike of 1953. In 1959 he was transferred to Thambani mission where he retired in 1975. He now lives a few meters away from the mission.

(b). H. Mletseni

He came to the mission in the early 1950s as a young man to attend the primary school. Since his father died when he was young, he began to fend for himself early. At the mission, he worked as payment for his school fees. Because of his hard work, he became a favourite of Fields. Fields taught him many industrial skills. In 1960, he married the second born daughter of another of Fields' best African workers, J. Khwangwala. He has worked all his life at Matandani mission except for a few years when he went for a gardening course at Solusi mission and worked at Malamulo College. Today, he is retired and resides near the Matandani mission.

(c). Mrs. Ethel Botomani

The first-born daughter of Pastor J. Khwangwala now married to Mr Botomani, the brother of the first African President of the Malawi Union, F. Botomani (1926-1998). She grew up mostly at Matandani mission during the era of Fields. Her father being a favourite African co-worker of Fields, Ethel and her siblings played with the Fields' three children, Webster, Davies and Bargeline. She now lives in Mwanza where she is also a *nyakwawa* (head of a village ward).

(d). M. Nzume

Born in 1941 at Likoma Island, he came to Neno in 1962. On 9th November 1963 O.I. Fields employed him as a domestic servant. When Fields left in 1967, he was taken by Cronje and worked as a domestic servant as well. After the departure of Cronje, he was employed as a casual worker on the mission. Today, he lives in Samson village near Matandani mission.

(e). S. J. Kaphale

He was born in 1932 and attended his primary education at Matandani mission. Fellow classmates included B. Makala who headed the Industrial School between 1979 and 1980 and Mr Kafaliana. His father, J. Kaphale also attended Matandani mission school in the early 1920s and was at one time taught dyeing and cloth-making skills by Wilfred Gudu, a demoted teacher at the mission at that time. S.J. Kaphale worked as a teacher in the government between 1960 and 1985. Today he lives in retirement on the outskirts of the mission.

(f). B. Thyoka

Now a maintenance supervisor in charge of the carpentry shop, at Matandani mission, B. Thyoka was born in 1947. Between 1968 and 1970 he attended the industrial school where he specialized in carpentry and joinery. He worked in government and private firms before joining Matandani mission in the capacity mentioned above. When the junior secondary school opened in 1969, he was one of the first students.

(g). S.F. Machilika

Now the registrar of the school, he attended part of his primary school education at the mission in the 1960s when O.I. Fields was the director. He worked for many years as a primary school teacher, rising to the position of Head while working at Soche Primary School. After a short break of four years (1985-1989) when he attended Solusi University, he taught first at Matandani, then at Malamulo before going back to Matandani where he is currently (2000) working.

ii. List of Mission Directors and Principals

Mission Directors during in the Missionary Era (1908-1971)

Missionary	Period Served	Home Country
S.M. Konigmacher	1908-1914	America
H.J. Hurlow	1915-1917 1919-1920	America
Moses Chauluka and K.M. Malinki*	1917-1919	Malawi
G.A. Ellingworth	1920-1923	England
W.L. Davy	1923-1925	Canada
W.L. Davy (second time)	1927-1934	Canada
E.B. Jewell	1934-1937	America
Y. Sosola*	1937-1938	Malawi
B.L. Ellingworth	1938-1939	England
O.I. Fields	1943-1967	America
K.B. Cronje	1968-1970	America
M.O. Klausen	1970-1971	America

* Indicates Temporary African Directors

Mission Principals during the Era of National Leadership (1971-1989)

Principal	Period Served	Country/ethnicity
T. Nkungula	1971-1975	Malawi – Ngoni

O.R. Follet	1976-1977	America
Fischer	Jan 1977 – May 1977	America
M.T. Kachoka (Acting)	May 1977–end 1977	Malawi-Ngoni
W.W. Khonje	1977 - 1979	Malawi-Ngoni
M. Sosola	1979 – 1984	Malawi-Ngoni
E. Kamwendo	1984 – 1987	Malawi-Ngoni
G.H. Kunkhoma	1987 – 1988	Malawi-Ngoni
E.Y. Ntata	1988 – 1989	Malawi-Ngoni
B.D. Kadzombe	1989 1996	Malawi-Ngoni

Note the number of Ngoni Principals

iii. Industrial School Student Enrolment (1953-1989)

Period of Study	Number Enrolled	Foreign Students
1953-1957	1	-
1954-1958	2	1: Zambia
1955-1959	4	-
1957-1961	4	-
1958-1962	5	1: Zambia
1959-1963	6	-
1962-1965	8	1: Tanzania
1964-1965	8	-
1965-1968	5	-
1967-1969	3	-
1968-1970	6	-
1970-1971	13	1: Botswana
1971-1972	8	-
1972-1973	6	-

1973-1974	8	-
1974-1975	5	-
1975-1976	6	-
1976-1977	8	-
1977-1978	5	-
1978-1979	5	-
1979-1980	5	-
1980-1981	7	-
1981-1982	6	-
1982-1983	6	1: Uganda
1983-1988	No record of student enrollment	
1988-1989	4	-

Bibliography

PRIMARY SOURCES

Oral Informants

S.J. Kaphale, born in 1932 and attended Matandani mission school where he later taught. He is retired and lives at Chakulemeka village.

P. Sosola, born 1935, is son of Pastor Y. Sosola. Mr P. Sosola is the in-charge of Matandani dispensary and maternity.

F.L. Matsimbe, born in 1911 and attended Matandani mission school where he later taught. He is retired and lives in the vicinity of the mission.

B. L. Chipazo born about 1945 attended the industrial school. He lives not far away from the mission.

B. Thyoka, born in 1947 attended the industrial school. He is currently a carpentry foreman at the mission's maintenance section.

S.F. Machilika is currently the Registrar of Matandani mission secondary school.

M. Nzume, formerly a domestic worker of both Fields and Cronje, worked for many years (until 1999) as a messenger at the mission. He and his family reside at Samson village.

Mrs Nzume, wife to M. Nzume. She resides at Samson village where she helps her husband in subsistence farming.

M.F. Nseula, retired head teacher of Matandani Primary School and for a long time a worker at the Voice of Prophecy in Blantyre. He resides at Nseula village.

Mrs. E. Botomani is the first-born daughter of Pastor J. Khwangwala. She currently resides in Mwanza district with her family.

Mrs. Mletseni is the wife of Mr H. Mletseni and sister to Mrs. E. Botomani. She is also the daughter of Pastor Khwangwala. She works at Matandani mission dispensary.

Mrs. Machilika is the wife of Mr. S. Machilika and currently a primary school teacher at Matandani Mission Primary School.

H. Mletseni has worked for many years at Matandani mission in various capacities, as a driver, industrial school tutor and boarding master.

Mr Beer is the one who is in charge of water maintenance at the mission. He was one of the people who witnessed and took part in the building of the water canal.

H. Chinsinga is the first-born son of B. Chinsinga. He currently runs his own vehicle maintenance shop in Gaborone, Botswana.

Mrs. G. Nzabonimpaye, born 1966, is the daughter of the late Pastor W.W. Khonje. Mrs. Nzabonimpaye works as a teacher at Thamaga Community Junior Secondary, Botswana.

Mrs Esmie Kaphale, a farmer (about 60 years old), is the grand daughter of Mark Chakachadza the initiator in the establishment of Matandani mission. She resides at Chakulemeka village, near Matandani mission.

Pastor Malopa is the current president of the Malawi Union.

Pastor H. Nyirenda is a teacher at Matandani Secondary School.

Pastor K. Bilima is the current Education Director in the Malawi Union.

Matandani Papers (MP)

Internal memo from the Deputy Principal, M.T. Kachoka, to the Assistant Deputy Principal, Pastor D. M. Masinga, July 1977.

Letter from H.G. Kamwendo Principal Matandani Mission to the Education Director, South East Africa Union, 25 September 1986.

Letter from H.P. Williams, Secretary of the Beit Trust headquarters, England, to Mr Nkungula, Principal of Matandani Mission, 17 December 1973.

Letter from H.P. Williams, Secretary of the Beit Trust headquarters, England to Mr Nkungula, Principal of Matandani mission, 17 December 1973.

Letter from J.H. Ingham, Beit Trust representative in Rhodesia to the Principal, Matandani Training School, 4 October 1975.

Letter from J.H. Ingham, Beit Trust representative in Rhodesia to the Principal, Matandani Training School 14 October 1975.

Letter from J.H. Ingham, Beit Trust representative in Rhodesia to the principal, Matandani Training School, 17 May 1977.

Letter from the Ministry of Labour, Superintendent of Trade Tests to the Principal, Matandani Training School, 5 August 1982.

Letter from the principal Matandani Training School to Mr LM Mabunya of Lakeview mission, 20 February 1976.

Letter from the principal of Matandani H.G. Kamwendo to C. Patterson, Director of ADRA department, Eastern Africa Division, Harare, 17 January 1985.

Letter from W. Duncan Eve, Secretary General Conference of Seventh-day Adventists, Southern Africa Division to Students, Industrial and maintenance course, Matandani mission, 13 April 1964.

Matandani Training School Examination results for 1985.
Matandani Training School memo: 1985/86 unusually large expenses.
Minutes of the Matandani Industrial School, Blantyre, 22 December 1966.
Minutes of the Matandani Training School Board meeting held at Matandani mission, 28 June 1972.
Minutes of the Matandani Training School Board meeting held in Blantyre on 2 November 1971.
Minutes of the Matandani Training School Board meetings held at Matandani mission, 28 June 1972.
Minutes of the Matandani Training School Board, 10 June 1976.
Minutes of the Matandani Training School Board, Blantyre, December 1980.
Minutes of the South East Africa Union, sub-committee on Education: Goals and Objectives, 13 October 1977.
Minutes of the special meeting to discuss the future of the Industrial School, 10 March 1971.
Minutes of the special meeting to discuss the future of the Industrial School, 10 March 1971.
Minutes of the Matandani Training School on Campus Board, 3 April 1986.

Malawi Union Matandani Papers (MUMP)

Matandani Training School Board minutes of year-end meeting, 9 December 1987.
Matandani Training School Board of available members held in Blantyre on 27 October 1986.
Minutes of a meting of the sub-committee on the future of Matandani Training School held in Blantyre on 17 April 1989.
Minutes of Matandani Training School on Campus Board meeting, 3 April 1989.
Minutes of Matandani Training School on Campus mid-year Board meeting, 29 March 1988.
Minutes of Matandani Training School year-end Board meeting, 8 November 1988.
Minutes of Matandani Training School year-end meeting, 8 November 1988

Archival Sources – Malawi National Archives, Zomba (MNA)

District Commissioner's Notes, Neno (Central Shire District), 1 March, 1907- 31 March 1950.

District Commissioner's Notes. Neno (Central Shire), District Book Volume 11, 20 August 1918 to 17 January 1923.
File number 56/SDB/1/12/1 on the Seventh-day Adventists conflict with remnants of the Seventh-Day Baptists in Northern Malawi.
The Good File, S43/1/18/1 covering the activities of Wilfred Gudu of the "Ana a Mulungu Church."
Neno (Central Shire) District Book, Volume II, 1 April 1923-31 March 1928.

Ellen G. White Estate Papers (EWEP)

"History of the South East Africa Union," 1952 (typescript, no author).
Robinson, V, "Third Angel over Africa", (typescript, no date).
Maxwell S.G, *I Loved Africa*, January 1976, (typescript).

Miscellaneous Papers (MiP)

General Conference Bulletin, volume 7, 3 June 1913.
Deed of sale, the registrar of the high court, Blantyre and J.C. Rogers 19 December 1907."
Matandani School Prospectus, 1998 (draft).
Matandani Training School. (a two-page undated document).
Matandani Mission Prospectus, 1979/80"
Malamulo General School Prospectus 1987/88."
Seventh-day Adventist Yearbook, Washington: Review and Herald Publishing Association, 1991.
The History of Pastor K.M. Malinki (an autobiographical sketch)."

SECONDARY SOURCES

Unpublished

Appel, D., "The Effect of the Depression on the SDA Church," term paper, Andrews University, USA (no date).
Bilima, J, "James Malinki of Malawi: Church Leader in Cross-Cultural Ministry," DMin, Andrews University, USA, 1993.
Bilima, J, "The Seventh-day Adventist Church in Malawi, 1900-1980," MDiv, Andrews University, USA, 1987.
Boeder, Robert B., "Malawians Abroad: The History of Labour Migration from Malawi to its Neighbours 1891-1914," PhD, University of Michigan, 1974.
Boeder, Robert B., "Wilfrid Good and Ana a Mulungu Church," History seminar paper, University of Malawi, Chancellor College, Zomba, 1982/83.
Doss, Gordon, "Survey of the Organizational Development and Growth of the South East Africa Union," BA research paper for the course History of the Seventh-day Adventist Church (CH 570), Andrews University, May 1974.
Khanje, Cedric, "Impact of Malamulo Mission in Southern Malawi, Thyolo 1902-1972: A Broad Perspective," Seminar paper, University of Malawi, Chancellor College, 1972.
Masuku, S.J, "New Approaches for Seventh-day Adventist Evangelism in Swaziland," DMin, Andrews University, 1996.
Matemba, Y. H, "Joseph Booth: A Critical Look at his Association with the Seventh-day Adventist Church in Malawi, 1892-1906."
Matemba, Yonah H, "The Practice of Rebaptism in the SDA Church," MA module, University of Malawi, Department of Theology and Religious Studies, May 1997.
Matemba, Yonah H, "Aspects of Seventh-day Adventist Church Polity: The Case of the Malawi Union," MA module, University of Malawi, Department of Theology and Religious Studies, May 1998.
Murowa, E.P.P., "Reverend Albert Kambuwa: A Critical Analysis of His Writings," History Seminar Paper, University of Malawi, Chancellor College, 1976-1977.
Musowa, E.P.P., "The Ana a Mulungu Church of Wilfred Gudu: Its Raison d' Etre," Theology seminar paper, University of Malawi, Chancellor College, Zomba, 1981.
Mvundura, Elijah, "Separation of Church and State," 1999 (draft document).
Mvundura, Elijah, "The Great Controversy: A Historiographical Review", 1999 (draft document).

Sayenda, S.K., "Missionaries and Health: The Case of Malamulo Mission Hospital, 1907-1964," History Seminar Paper, Chancellor College, University of Malawi, 1990.
Schwarz, Richard, "John Harvey Kellogg: An American Reformer," Ph.D., University of Michigan, USA, 1964.
Thapelo, T, "The Political Economy of Stratified Distribution in Rural Botswana, 1966-1996: State, Peasants and Agro-Pastoral Reform," PhD, University of London, School of Oriental and African Studies, 1998.
Yokasi, S.K., "An Evaluation of Seventh-day Adventist Mission in the Education Field from 1907 to the present," University of Malawi, Chancellor College, 1980.

Published

Amayo, Gershom, "Seventh-day Adventist Contribution to Kenya," in Pfeiffer (ed.) *Seventh-day Adventist Contributions*, p. 61).
Atkinson, R.J., *Knowledge and Explanation in History: An Introduction to the Philosophy of History*, London: Macmillan, 1978, pp. 79-88.
Bediako, M, " Miracle in Southern Africa," *The Advent Review*, 6 February 1992.
Booth, Joseph, *Africa for the Africans*, (ed. Laura Perry), Blantyre: CLAIM-Kachere, ³1998 (1897).
Chakanza, J. Chaphadzika, *Voices of Preachers in Protest: The Ministry of Two Malawian Prophets: Elliot Kamwana and Wilfred Gudu*, Blantyre: CLAIM-Kachere, 1998.
Chakanza, J., Chaphadzika, 'Sectarianism in Joseph Booth's Mission Foundations. The Search for Causative Factors," *Religion in Malawi*, No. 2, Vol. 1, November 1988.
Chakanza, J., Chaphadzika, "An Annotated List of Independent Churches in Malawi 1900-1981," *Sources for the Study of Religion in Malawi*, No. 10, December 1983.
Chirwa, RM., "Politics in the Cartoon in Malawi: The Democrat Cartoons," in Kings Phiri. and Kenneth Ross (eds.), *Democratization in Malawi: A Stocktaking*, Blantyre: CLAIM-Kachere, 1998.
Doss, Gordon, "George James: Pioneer in Malawi Work", *Adventist Review*, 1993.
Edwards, Josephine C., "Graduation at Malamulo," *The Youth's Instructor*, 2 October 1951.
Fiedler, Klaus, "Christian Missions and Western Colonialism: Soulmates or Antagonists?" in Kenneth Ross (ed.), *Faith at the Frontiers of Knowledge*, Blantyre: CLAIM-Kachere, 1998.

BIBLIOGRAPHY 149

Fiedler, Klaus, "The 'Smaller' Churches and 'Big' Government," in Matembo S. Nzunda and Kenneth R. Ross, *Church, Law and Political Transition in Malawi 1992-94*, Gweru: Mambo, 1995, pp. 166-168.

Fiedler, Klaus, *Christianity and African Culture: Conservative German Protestant Missionaries in Tanzania, 1900-1940*, Blantyre: CLAIM-Kachere, 1999.

Fiedler, Klaus, *The Story of Faith Missions*, Oxford: Regnum, 1994.

Insight Magazine, 23 June 1990.

Kalilombe, P.A., *Doing Theology at the Grassroots: Theological Essays from Malawi*, Mambo: Gweru, 1999.

Kazembe, Boyd, "Bangwe SDA Church Closure Revisited," *The Nation*, 14 April 2000.

Langworthy, Harry, *"Africa for the Africans": The Life of Joseph Booth*, Blantyre: CLAIM-Kachere, 1996.

Leeds, Paul, *Practical Research: Planning and Design*, New York: Macmillan, 1985, p. 125.

Livingstone, D., *Missionary Travels and Researches in South Africa*, London: John Murray; New York: Harper Brothers, 1858.

Loughborough, J.N., *The Second Advent Movement: Its Rise and Progress*, Washington: Review and Herald Publishing Association, 1992.

Matemba, Yonah H., "Some Aspects of the History of the Seventh-day Adventists in Botswana from 1922 to 1970," *Botswana Notes and Records*, Vol. 29, 1997.

Monterrey, "Waco: Insights on the Davidian Movement part 1," *Our Firm Foundation*, volume 8, Number 6, June 1993.

Mwansa, G., "Zimbabwe Union Conference: A Pride of Eastern Africa Division," *Outlook*, volume 17, number 3, July-September 1999.

Mwasi, Y. Z., *Essential and Paramount Reasons for Working Independently*, Blantyre: CLAIM-Kachere, 1999.

Ncozana, S., *Sangaya: A Leader in the Synod of Blantyre Church of Central Africa Presbyterian*, Blantyre: CLAIM-Kachere, (second edition, revised), 1999.

Needham, D.E., *Iron Age to Independence: A History of Central Africa*, London: Longman, 1974.

Northup, N., "The Migrations of the Yao and Kololo into Southern Malawi: Aspects of Migrations in Nineteenth Century Africa, *International Journal of African Studies*, vol. 19, no. 1 (1986), pp. 55-75.

Nzunda, Matembo. and Kenneth R. Ross (eds.), *Church, Law and Political Transition in Malawi 1992-94*, Gweru: Mambo, 1995.

Our Firm Foundation, volume 8, number 6, June 1993.

Pfeiffer, B. (ed.), *Seventh-day Adventist Contributions to East Africa 1903-1983*, Frankfurt: Peter Lang, 1985.
Pfeiffer, Baldur E., "The Coming of the Mission to East Africa", in Baldur E. Pfeiffer (ed.), *Seventh-day Adventist Contribution to East Africa, 1903-1983*, Frankfurt: Peter Lang, 1985.
Phiri, Isabel, Kenneth Ross and Jim Cox (eds.)., *The Role of Christianity in Development, Peace and Reconstruction: Southern Perspectives*, Nairobi: All Africa Conference of Churches, Kolbe Press, 1996.
Phiri, Kings and Kenneth Ross (eds.), *Democratization in Malawi: A Stocktaking*, Blantyre: CLAIM-Kachere, 1998.
Pride Magazine (second edition), 1999.
Reich, Jeff, "A.T. Jones and the Church," *Our Firm Foundation*, vol. 7, no. 11, pp. 4-7.
Reijnaerts, Hubert, Ann Nielsen and Matthew Schoffeleers, *Montfortians: Their Spirituality and Pastoral Approach*, Blantyre: CLAIM-Kachere, 1997.
Ross, Andrew C., *Blantyre Mission and the Making of Modern Malawi*, Blantyre: CLAIM-Kachere, 1996.
Ross, Kenneth R., (ed.)., *Christianity in Malawi; A Source Book*, Gweru: Mambo, 1996.
Ross, Kenneth R., (ed.)., *Faith at the Frontiers of Knowledge*, Blantyre: CLAIM-Kachere, 1998.
Rotberg, Robert (ed.), *Hero of the Nation. Chipembere of Malawi. An Autobiography*, Blantyre: CLAIM-Kachere, 2001.
Rotberg, Robert, *The Rise of Nationalism in Central Africa: The Making of Malawi and Zambia: 1873-1964*, Cambridge, Massachusetts: Harvard University Press, 1967.
Schwarz, R.W., *Light Bearers to the Remnant*, California: Pacific Press, 1979.
Seventh-day Adventist Yearbook (1971), Washington: Review and Herald Publishing Association.
Seventh-day Adventist Church Manual (revised 1995 edition), Maryland: Review and Herald Publishing Association.
Shepperson, George and Tom Price, *Independent African: John Chilembwe and the Nyasaland Rising of 1915*, Edinburgh: Edinburgh University Press, ^{5}1987 (1958), reprinted Blantyre: CLAIM-Kachere, ^{6}2000.
White, E.G., *Education*, Mount View, California: Pacific Press Publishing House, 1952.
White, Ellen G., *Ministry of Healing*, Mountain View, California: Pacific Press, 1913.
White, Ellen G., *The Great Controversy*, Ottawa: Pacific Press, 1993 (1888).

www.ingramcontent.com/pod-product-compliance
Lightning Source LLC
Chambersburg PA
CBHW021759230426
43669CB00006B/133